DATE DUE			
MAY 28 '82			
FEB 18 1987			
AUG 2 2 1989			
JUL 2 6 1995			
NOV 2 6 1996			
NOV 0 5 2003			
APR 2 9			

SOCIAL WELFARE
IN THE SOUTH

SOCIAL WELFARE IN THE SOUTH

From Colonial Times to World War I

Elizabeth Wisner

LOUISIANA STATE UNIVERSITY PRESS

Baton Rouge

Library of Congress Catalog Card Number 78–123206
ISBN–0–8071–0505–8
Manufactured in the United States of America by
The TJM Corporation, Baton Rouge, Louisiana

Designed by Jules B. McKee

PREFACE

HISTORICAL STUDIES of the South, of the Civil War, and of its aftermath are voluminous, and they continue to be written and the events reinterpreted. In contrast, there is little published material on Southern social welfare developments. This lack is unfortunate for students of social work, especially Southern students, who need to understand the background of present-day programs. Although the historical background of modern social services is presumably an important subject in the education of social workers, especially at the doctoral level, to many students past movements often seem irrelevant to the complex milieu to which they are introduced during their professional education. They must acquire not only new knowledge but new techniques. Furthermore, there is a growing body of professional literature on current issues and practice to engage their time and interest. Social work education ought to be geared to the acquisition of knowledge for use, and the title of a volume by the historian Henry Steele Commager—*The Search for a Usable Past* —is a reminder that social welfare history should serve this purpose.

The period from the colonial settlements to World War

I was chosen for this study because the economic and social institutions of the Old South set that region apart from the rest of the nation and cast a long shadow on those services of traditional concern to the social worker. This book is in no sense a definitive account of all aspects of the subject. The reader will note that the care of dependent and neglected children, always a major social problem in the South, has been largely excluded here, as has a full description of measures to provide for handicapped groups. Instead, emphasis has been placed on the basic problem of poverty and the treatment of those in need of public aid—a large segment of the population. Further research is necessary before a more comprehensive Southern social welfare history can be written.

The author wishes to express appreciation to many former students of the Tulane University School of Social Work for the historical material made available in the form of their M.S. theses. Subjects such as the old poor laws and historical studies in general are not particularly appealing to graduate students geared to problems which they meet in current practice. However, once a subject was mutually agreed on, the students were conscientious and energetic in searching through statutes, legislative documents, agency reports, and other source material related to their topics. That these theses have been invaluable to the author is evident in the bibliographical essay. I am also grateful to the late Mrs. Berthe T. Heineberg for her careful checking and patience in retyping the several drafts of this manuscript.

CONTENTS

SOCIAL WELFARE
IN THE SOUTH

INTRODUCTION
Early Measures for the Relief of the Poor

THE SOUTH as a geographic region has often been spoken of as though there were a "solid South," although there are several different Souths today. In this study the eleven states that seceded from the Union to form the Confederacy have been included for reasons that will appear evident. These were the states where the institution of slavery largely molded a stratified economic and social order, and where the Civil War wrought its greatest misery and destruction. The political turmoils during the period of Reconstruction also left a mark on the outlook and the attitudes of the people. These historical facts were to characterize the South as different from the rest of the nation, and any discussion of poverty and the social welfare measures instituted on behalf of the poor must take them into consideration.

The old statewide poor laws, which made mandatory the support of the poor by local government units, the towns or the counties, have occasionally been described as our first form of social security. Their failure to provide adequate relief or care in countless jurisdictions has been recorded in many studies. To restate the theory of public aid: it required that the taxpayers of each local community must provide the necessaries of life for the destitute. The poor law was a part of the English governmental system brought to this country by the early settlers. Such provisions were first embodied in the legislation of the colonies along the Atlantic coast and later spread to the new territories and states. This principle of local responsibility is referred to as the first plank in the poor laws. However, to protect local taxpayers and to make some poor persons ineligible for local relief, the laws provided certain regulations, namely, settlement and family responsibility. The provisions for "settlement," or residence in a town or county for a specific period of time, may be regarded as the second plank in the poor laws. Such regulations varied among the colonies. The accompanying procedure for removing relief applicants without a settlement to the communities where they presumably belonged was a troublesome aspect of many poor laws.

The effect of these requirements was often to deny assistance to persons in need because they had not resided the requisite number of years in a new locality and had lost their former settlement in a jurisdiction to which they might be removed by the poor law authorities. Mobility of population is not a new phenomenon in America. As early as the colonial period, many families moved about to seek a livelihood, or in some instances to secure medical care, or to join relatives. The town was the unit of administration in the New England states and all persons had to have a settlement in a particular town. The poor law records are strewn with references to "strangers"—often persons who had come from nearby localities, therefore having no settlement in the town to which they wished to move. Attempts to legislate against the settlement of such persons was in part due to fear that their religious and political views might prove disturbing to local tranquility. In the long run, however, it was the fear that they might become dependent and a burden on the local taxpayers that led to the stiffening of the residence requirements and the increasing complexity of the New England poor laws.

The settlement proviso incorporated in most state public assistance laws continued for many years to be an obstacle in meeting the needs of families who did not meet the residence requirement of the particular state in which they were living. In view of the recent United States Supreme Court decision *Shapiro* v. *Thompson*,[1] which outlaws residence as an eligibility requirement for public assistance and which has ended the long struggle on the part of public welfare officials and social workers to abolish such restrictions, a brief reference to past efforts seems timely. Among proposals to reform the settlement requirement had been that of a uniform law to lessen the problems created by the different lengths of residence required by the states. In 1790, little Rhode Island, the last of the thirteen colonies to ratify the Constitution of the new republic, submitted an amendment to the proposed Constitution, to provide that Congress should have

[1] *Shapiro* v. *Thompson,* 394 U. S. 618 (1969).

the power to establish a uniform rule of inhabitancy and settlement of the poor for the various states of the Union. This proposal was unique since it suggested a radical departure from the legislation in the colonies. There were no reasons given for this resolution, but since the Rhode Island Committee on Amendments had received instructions from the towns, it may be assumed that the complexities of the settlement laws had proved burdensome. Uniform settlement legislation provided by Congress would not have solved all problems created by the early settlement laws, but the influence of federal legislation would have been far-reaching.

There have been subsequent proposals that the uniformity of these laws be secured by means of federal legislation and occasional appeals to abolish all settlement laws. After the decades of discouraging attempts to mitigate the effect of residence legislation on the needs of many poor persons, the recent Supreme Court decision outlawing such statutes is heartening. It is also a reminder of a prediction made in 1940 by Edith Abbott, an outstanding critic of the poor laws and of modern residence requirements:

The improvements in the standards of social work which come into conflict with archaic laws must eventually effect considerable changes in the settlement laws. When such changes occur in legislation they frequently come suddenly, although they may have been preceded by a period in which the trend actually appeared to be for a time in another direction. The wheels of social change grind slowly at times, and then they may turn with fantastic speed. The wide recognition of the need for a change in the system of settlement laws cannot but have its ultimate effect upon both practice and legislation.[2]

To go back to basic principles embodied in the poor laws which were enforced in some states, family responsibility—the statutory obligation of certain members of the family to support their destitute relatives—was the third plank in such legislation. Local officials had to call on family members able to provide support and might prosecute those who refused to assume such responsibility. Although the duty of children to support their aged parents may still be a matter of controversy in some states in connection with old-age assistance, the general effect of the family responsibility provisions on the administration of modern public assistance programs has not been as critical as that of the residence laws, and therefore the question will not be reviewed in this brief discussion of modern public aid provisions.

Poverty, in contrast to *destitution*, is of course a relative term, and a definition of the poor was not (and probably could not be) incorporated in the acts. Such terms as "the poor," "the impotent," and "the infirm" were widely used to describe those eligible for poor relief. On the whole there was acceptance that this group constituted "the deserving poor." The so-called able-

[2] Edith Abbott, *Public Assistance* (Chicago: University of Chicago Press, 1940), 189–90. The best analysis and critique of the American poor laws are to be found in this volume.

bodied poor who were unable to find employment or
were destitute for other reasons were frequently classi-
fied as among the "undeserving poor"; there was a continuing dilemma as to whether or not, and under what
circumstances, they should be aided from public funds.
A committee appointed by the Massachusetts general
court wrestled with this question in 1821. Under the
leadership of Josiah Quincy, its chairman, this committee
reported on the state's pauper laws. Fear that relief to
the able-bodied would destroy the economical habits of
the laboring class was foremost in the minds of the committee members, but the difficulty of discriminating
between the needs of the able-bodied poor and "the impotent" was recognized: "This difficulty cannot apparently be removed by any legislative provision. There must
be in the nature of things, numerous and minute shades of
difference between the pauper who, through impotency,
can do absolutely nothing and the pauper who is able to
do something, but that, very little. . . ." The report continued, "There must always exist so many circumstances
of age, sex, previous habits, muscular or mental strength,
to be taken into account that society is absolutely incapa-
ble to fix any standard or to prescribe any rule by which
the claim of right to the benefit of public provision shall
be absolutely determined." [3] Thus, as the report points

[3] Massachusetts General Court, Committee on Pauper Laws,
Report of Committee to Whom Was Referred the Consideration
of the Pauper Laws of the Commonwealth, 1821, reprinted
in Sophonisba P. Breckinridge, *Public Welfare Administration*

out, determination of "who are the poor" must be left to the discretion of local officials, a system often resulting in unequal treatment of the destitute in the South as well as the North.

The Social Security Act of 1935 is now regarded as a historic piece of social legislation which has in many respects revolutionized the old poor law systems. Probably in no section of the country has the impact of federal funds and federal standards in the administration of public assistance and child welfare programs been greater than in the Southern region. As many specialists in Southern history have emphasized, poverty was a continuous and widespread feature of the Southern experience since the early years of the Civil War. In his message to a conference in 1938 on economic conditions in the South, President Franklin Roosevelt stated that the region was "the Nation's No. 1 economic problem—the Nation's problem, not merely the South's." The National Emergency Council's *Report on Economic Conditions of the South,* which was submitted to the President, included data on the retarded economic conditions—little industry, low wages, and lack of purchasing power—and pointed to the tenant-farm arrangement, which resulted in an average annual gross income in 1929 of $186, as compared with $528 for other American farmers. At the same time the South educated (or failed to educate)

---

in the United States (2nd ed.; Chicago: University of Chicago Press, 1938), 30–37.

one-third of the nation's children with one-sixth of the nation's school revenues. Southern rates of syphilis, pellagra, and tuberculosis were higher than in other sections of the country. It is not surprising that the President's concern over "one-third of a nation ill-housed, ill-clad, ill-nourished" lingered in the memory of those persons concerned with the poor of the South. Long before the Civil War or the Depression of the 1930's—in fact from the beginning of the colonial settlements—the destitute, the sick, the aged, and orphaned children are recorded as needing public aid.

I

The Colonial Period

SOUTHERN SOCIAL WELFARE history begins with the early public provisions for the poor in Virginia, and such legislation in the first colonial settlement bore the earmarks of the Elizabethan poor laws, as did the provisions in the New England colonies. Similar relief measures were enacted in the colonies of North and South Carolina. The grandiose experiment in philanthropy led by General James Oglethorpe which resulted in the founding of the Georgia colony also belongs in this period. In Georgia, local officials maintained a commissary from which newly arrived settlers could draw supplies, and this served as a substitute for public aid during the administration of the colony by the London trustees.

Unlike the New England colonies—where the administration of relief was from the beginning a civil function, with town officials, the selectmen, or overseers responsible for the care of the poor—in Virginia and the Carolinas the Anglican clergy served in this capacity, with the parish as the local governmental unit. Among the public duties of the vestries, acting through the church wardens, was the responsibility for calling attention to

cases of extreme poverty and providing for such persons
at the expense of the parish. Georgia, after the termina-
tion of the colonial charter in 1752, also enacted a poor
law, which was administered by church authorities under
the provincial government.

That the early parish records in Virginia contain numerous references to the poor in need of aid is perhaps
not surprising in view of the situation of a large number
of immigrants to the new settlement. Poverty and unemployment were widespread in England, and many persons deprived of a means of livelihood were sent to Virginia as indentured servants. They formed the chief source
of labor during the seventeenth century, just as Negro
slaves did during the next century. Many social problems
inevitably developed. A general poor law passed in 1642–
43, defining the duties of the vestries, stated that poverty
had long existed in the colony; the act recognized that
sickness and old age prevented many inhabitants from
working. There are complaints in the records about the
great increase in the number of "vagabonds, idle and dissolute persons," who ran away from their families and
left their wives and children dependent on the parishes
for support.

A considerable body of legislation was passed for the
care of poor illegitimate and orphaned children between
1647 and 1769. The system of "binding out," or apprenticeship, was the chief method of providing for such children. With the lack of other child care and training resources, apprenticeship under a conscientious master was

a means of providing the child with an opportunity to learn a trade. There was also the idea that the religious and moral behavior of these children would be improved. Obviously, not all masters lived up to the ideal, and abuses were inevitable. Children whose parents were considered "idle, dissolute and disorderly persons" could under the laws be bound out by the church wardens on a certificate of the county courts. The recurring references to "bastards" and later to the increase in the number of illegitimate mulatto children resulted in a series of laws governing illegitimacy. Widespread unemployment was not a major problem in the new colonies, as it had been in England, and there was less actual destitution. Yet the New World did not escape the fact of poverty or many of the social ills that had long plagued the Old World.

In South Carolina, a 1712 statute repealing an earlier poor law pointed to the increase of poverty in all parts of the colony and to the need for preventing "the perishing of the poor whether young or old for want of the supplies as are necessary." [1] As in Virginia, the parish vestries and wardens were responsible for the administration of poor relief; many of the same problems arose and the laws were frequently amended.

North Carolina before the Revolution presents a picture of extremely primitive living conditions, with the majority of the population existing so close to the edge of want that there was little interest in special legislation for "the poor." It was an area with small, widely scat-

[1] *Statutes of South Carolina* (1682–1716), 593–98.

tered settlements, no cities, poor roads, no newspapers, and many of the inhabitants illiterate. Finally, in 1755, an act was passed to restrain and punish vagrants and to provide for the poor. Vagrancy legislation was frequently linked with legal provisions for the poor, and the North Carolina act is fairly typical of many of the New England laws. All local inhabitants were forbidden to entertain or employ for more than forty-eight hours any taxable person removing from another parish, unless he had a certificate from the proper official of his parish that his taxes were paid. The act also provided that a "vagabond" (the term was undefined) had to furnish security or be bound out to service. If no one was willing to take him, he was to be whipped thirty-nine lashes on his bare back. Moreover, "persons likely to become chargeable" (a phrase that runs throughout much of the New England legislation)—that is, persons or families who appeared unable to make a living and therefore were possible applicants for relief—were to be removed to the localities where they presumably belonged. In case of illness which prevented their removal because of danger to life, the church wardens were authorized to provide for their maintenance and cure. After recovery, they were subject to removal to their place of legal settlement. This negative statute of 1755 was apparently interpreted as making the church wardens responsible for their own poor.

Later amendments to the poor law indicate that as in Virginia, many settlements in North Carolina failed to appoint vestries, thus providing no relief for the poor. The masses had little enthusiasm for the established church and saw no need for public relief. However, several acts refer to the extreme poverty in various parishes and the assembly continued to legislate for the appointment of the clergy and for provisions to aid the poor. As for dependent children, apprenticeship was the usual method of care in North Carolina as it was elsewhere. Legislation governing relief to the poor continued to be enacted in the latter half of the nineteenth and early twentieth centuries, but such measures were largely directed to the building of almshouses in the counties, rather than to any reform of the poor laws.

Georgia, the last of the Southern colonies to be settled, represented a unique experiment in philanthropy. The story of the founding of this colony is familiar, and only a brief review is needed here of aspects of the scheme which relate to the welfare of the immigrants. The idea of founding a colony south of the Carolinas was conceived by General Oglethorpe, a member of Parliament interested in prison reform; and John Perceval, earl of Egmont, a wealthy aristocrat interested in helping the poor of London. An investigation of conditions in the Fleet Street and Marshalea prisons, where many of the poor debtors of London were held, had aroused Oglethorpe's sympathetic interest. It was apparent to him that they had no way of discharging their debts and if released from prison could find no employment in London. In 1732, Parliament granted to Oglethorpe and Perceval

a royal charter giving them the privilege of founding a
colony in the New World. To administer the project,
twenty-one trustees were named in the charter—all men
who had been active in charitable endeavors and were
disinterested in any profitable advantage to themselves.
However, as practical men, important in the political
affairs of their nation, the trustees realized that a strong
colony of English settlers on the Savannah River would
protect the border from Indian, Spanish, and French in-
vasions and would at the same time enrich English trade.

Persons "in decayed circumstances and thereby disabled from following any business in England, who if in
debt had leave from their creditors to go, and such as
recommended by Ministers, Church Wardens and Overseers of their respective parishes" [2] were to be selected
for planting the colony to be called Georgia. The undertaking aroused widespread enthusiasm. Many people rea-
soned, Why spend £50 a year supporting a destitute family in England when barely twice that amount would make
them permanently self-supporting overseas? The project was uncommonly well publicized and sermons were
preached all over England appealing for gifts to help the
poor emigrate to the new colony. Considerable sums were
raised by private subscriptions, with the trustees, the East
India Company, and the Bank of England making contri-

[2] Quoted in Leslie E. Church, *Oglethorpe: A Study of Philanthropy in England and Georgia* (London: Epworth Press,
1932), 61.

butions. When voluntary funds proved insufficient, Parliament appropriated £130,000, the largest sum given to support any of the colonies.

The trustees considered the applicants for immigration, investigating their morals and the circumstances which had led to their distress. Two weeks before departure the names of prospective settlers were advertised in the London newspapers so that creditors and deserted wives might have proper warning. Altogether 114 men, women, and children made up the first group of settlers, which sailed November 17, 1732, on the good ship *Ann*. Others followed, sent out on the Charity Fund; additional groups included Highlanders, Protestant refugees from Europe, and persons who went at their own expense. Contrary to a persistent belief, not many imprisoned debtors were sent, and those chosen were regarded as promising settlers for the new colony. It is probable, though, that many of the London poor were ill equipped to undertake the hardships of planting a new colony in the South. Benjamin Franklin, who disapproved of the whole undertaking, gave some harsh comments on the settlers in his autobiography: "The settlement of that province has lately begun but instead of being made with hardy, industrious husbandmen, accustomed to labor, the only people fit for such enterprise, it was with families of broken shopkeepers and other insolvent debtors, many of indolent and idle habits; taken out of the jails, who, being set down in the woods, unqualified for clearing

land, and unable to endure the hardships of a new settlement, perished in large numbers, leaving many helpless
children unprovided for." [3]

None of the London trustees appointed to administer
this philanthropic venture had ever seen the territory to
be settled. They were bemused by the illusion of a land
where semitropical fruit grew wild, where flourishing
mulberry trees would support a prosperous silkworm industry, and where other crops, all beneficial to English
trade, could be easily cultivated. Sitting in London, they
had a clear picture of what the colony *ought* to be. Their
blueprint for its management included minute regulations
governing the distribution of land, methods of cultiva-
tion, and supervision of the morals of the settlers. During
the first year the colonists were to be supplied from the
commissary and the exact amounts of meat, corn, sugar,
soap, and other commodities to be given each able-bodied
man were specified in detail, as were the smaller rations
for women and children. As one writer has said, "Such
provisions for the emigrants to Georgia have more the
ring of a well run jail or of a mercenary army than of a

[3] *The Autobiography of Benjamin Franklin* (Boston and
New York: Houghton Mifflin Co., 1896), 132–33. Franklin had
little regard for the poor of England and thought only "the
whip of hunger" would drive them to work. He urged the
repeal of the poor laws as the solution for poverty and widespread
unemployment. Then, he said, "St. Monday and St. Tuesday
will cease to be holidays . . . industry will increase and with it
plenty." Sidney and Beatrice Webb, *English Poor Law History*
(London-New York-Toronto: Longmans, Green & Co., 1929),
I, 10–11.

colony of free men seeking their fortune in the new world." [4]

The death rate was high among the early Georgia settlers, and many social problems arose. A council in Savannah, appointed and controlled by the London trustees, took care of local matters. The minutes of these council meetings record instances of relief in kind being given to the aged and sick. Thomas Cautin, keeper of the commissary, served as welfare agent. The trustees, though far removed, showed some concern in their correspondence with him that care be taken of the poor and sick. They instructed Cautin that orphans were "to be put on the store" until old enough to be apprenticed. Children aged six years and older were to be employed in the fields picking cotton at wages of 4d. a day—an arrangement that militated against the protection or training which apprenticeship was supposed to provide for children.

Frequent complaints of neglect and mistreatment of children in Georgia led to the founding in 1738 of the first permanent institution of its kind in the country, the Bethesda orphanage near Savannah.[5] George Whitefield,

---

[4] Daniel J. Boorstin, *The Americans* (New York: Random House, 1958), 87.

[5] The Ursuline Convent in New Orleans, usually credited with being the first institution in this country for dependent children, was founded as an educational institution and only temporarily housed a group of orphans. (See Bibliographical Essay.) It should also be noted that the first *public* orphanage in this country was established in Charleston, South Carolina, in 1790—seventeen years before the incorporation of the first orphan asylum in New York City.

a celebrated orator and one of the founders of Methodism,
had visited the new colony. Moved by the miserable situation of the orphans and of the many children living in
poor families, he decided to build an orphanage where
they could be cared for. Back in London, he persuaded
the trustees to allot five hundred acres of land on which
to build an institution. Whitefield was granted "the power of collecting charities" to finance the project. He returned to Georgia to carry out his plan and to become
the first manager of Bethesda. Benjamin Franklin expressed disapproval of Whitefield's plan to build the orphanage on the edge of Savannah. He argued that because
of the high cost of building materials in the settlement,
the institution should be located in Philadelphia and
the children sent there. This idea Whitefield resolutely
opposed. He set out on his travels northward to collect
funds for the orphan home. Although Franklin had previously refused to contribute to the building, he happened to attend one of Whitefield's sermons and was so
moved by the oratory that he emptied his pockets of all
his coppers, silver, and gold. Whitefield was successful
in collecting funds on his travels and also received con-
tributions from England. He set about building the Great
House while the children lived in temporary buildings.
An infirmary was added, and the institution when com-
pleted served as a center for various charitable efforts.
Whitefield was interested not only in caring for neglected
children but also in saving souls. He recorded that several strangers were brought to God at Bethesda.

In his zeal to provide for neglected children, White-field went about gathering in all of them he could find in the colony. Boys were removed from their guardians and other children taken from families where they had been placed. Almost immediately he was in difficulty with the trustees over his program of forced labor of children in the fields. Finally, the trustees ordered that bailiffs were to have the sole power of placing children in the orphan-age and of removing them when they were considered old enough to work; the trustees issued other regulations in-tended to curb Whitefield's activities. The orphanage, however, apparently thrived and served a useful purpose in a period when other resources for the care and educa-tion of children were lacking. Bethesda still operates as a modern child care center with a substantial endow-ment and with a program of treatment for emotionally disturbed children.

The Georgia colonial project, which had been gen-erously supported by individual charity and public funds, came to a dismal end in 1752 when the London trustees relinquished the charter to the crown. Enthusiasm for this philanthropy had waned in England as the colony failed to become self-supporting. The many strictures laid down by the trustees had long handicapped its economic development. There was no self-government, and many colonists complained that they could not support their families on the allotted fifty acres of pine-barren land. The ill-conceived silk industry did not prosper and many settlers deserted to other colonies, hoping for greater freedom and better economic opportunities. The welfare agent, Thomas Cautin, pleased neither London nor the settlers in his administration of relief supplies and was reported to be the most hated man in the colony. Thus ended the great philanthropic venture launched with such enthusiasm in England. Georgia was left the poorest of the colonies when the charter was relinquished.

The provincial government which took over the administration of Georgia adopted the state religion of England and empowered the vestries and church wardens to assess rates for the relief of the poor, as in Virginia and the Carolinas. With the separation of church and state following the Revolution, the administration of poor relief in the four Southern colonies became the responsibility of the overseers of the poor, the wardens of the poor, or in the case of Georgia, the county courts. Church influence on the relief practices of these colonies appears to have been negligible. Unfortunately for the destitute of the region, many county officials failed to provide any more adequate relief than had been granted under the parish system of the Anglican Church.

II
Relief in the Territories and States

MEASURES FOR THE relief of destitute persons in the remaining Confederate states, except Louisiana, were embodied in the early statutes and in some constitutions. Actually, the three basic principles of this legislation were much the same as in the older colonies. The counties were required to maintain their own poor out of local tax funds, and some states had provisions for settlement and family or relative responsibility. The jurisdictions covered by these states were, for a long period, largely frontier areas with scattered populations and few cities of any size. As the general standard of living was low in much of the region, there is little evidence of interest in the poor law provisions. In pioneer settings families were expected to help each other rather than have recourse to public aid. The poor laws which were enacted in all these states merely made it mandatory on the local officials to aid their destitute from local tax funds. The Negro slave is not excluded in the language of the laws, but other regulations governed his status as the responsibility of his master. Therefore it can be assumed that the slaves, who became one-third or more of the population, were in fact excluded from aid under the poor laws. It is impossible to say to what extent free Negroes were aided after emancipation except through the temporary Freedmen's Bureau (see Chapter 5).

As elsewhere in the early period, there were no institutions to house the poor, the aged, the handicapped, the insane, or dependent children—except the local jail. "Outdoor relief," as it was called, or relief to recipients of public aid in their own homes, with relatives or persons paid to care for them, was the only provision available. This was followed by the nationwide swing to "indoor" care in the almshouse or poor farm as a more economical method of dealing with the destitute. Although the neglect of the poor and the harsh administration of the laws are emphasized in this study, the system must be viewed in the light of the attitudes of the period and the generally low standard of living throughout much of the Southern region. Any student of the American poor law will note that many technical aspects of such legislation have been omitted in this discussion. Only the more special features of the various state provisions have been included, as a detailed account of the minor differences, state by state, would be burdensome to the reader and would add little that is significant to the American history of aid to the destitute.

Tennessee, one of the older Southern states, dated back to 1796. Originally a part of North Carolina, Tennessee carried over the poor law legislation of that state but made the county courts and justices of the peace instead of the overseers of the poor responsible for the administration. The county courts necessarily extended over the territory and had power to appropriate funds and administer the affairs of the counties. After taking cognizance of all destitute persons in the county who were judged proper persons to be supported, they had the authority to levy a tax for their relief. There was considerable migration into the new territories and states from the eastern areas and the question arose as to whether the counties were to be responsible for *all* who came to settle in Tennessee. The law therefore defined *inhabitant* and fixed a one year's residence as qualifying the newcomer for public aid.

Here as elsewhere along the frontiers of the New World, it is well to remember, neighbors and friends helped those in need. The following statement from a Tennessee document records the fact that mutual aid in many instances helped sustain the inhabitant in a pioneer setting: "When necessary they would share with one another, their money, their clothes, provision, ammunition, tools, labor, or anything they might have. A settler's cabin was without money and without price, for the relief or assistance of any worthy man. If a man was sick, or unable from accident to care for his crop, his neighbors assembled and did the work for him, and went home thinking they had done only a neighborly act." [1]

[1] Quoted in Ellen Barbour Wallace, "History of Legal Provisions for the Poor and of Public Welfare Administration in Tennessee" (M.S. thesis, School of Social Service Administration, University of Chicago, 1927), 9.

Moreover, the pioneer family was usually a unified group, tied together by common hardships. This fact may account for the lack of family or relative responsibility clauses in the poor laws of many Southern states. At least, the family solidarity that prevailed explained the lack of such a provision in the early Tennessee legislation.

Of all Southern states, Louisiana was in many respects unique. Although twice governed by France (and once by Spain), it did not adopt the highly centralized system of public relief or the concept of *droit d'assistance* conceived by the États-Generaux under Napoleon. Likewise, Louisiana inherited none of the English poor law influence transplanted to Virginia and the other colonies. W. C. C. Claiborne, the first governor of the Louisiana territory, who was a Virginian and politically active, was undoubtedly familiar with the poor law legislation in his home state. He urged the territorial legislature of Louisiana to make provisions for the poor, but to no avail. The new American government was unpopular with the older French citizens, and Claiborne faced many difficulties in trying to secure measures which differed from the previous mixture of French and Spanish administration and law.

In 1817 a bill to provide relief for the poor of the state failed to pass in the legislature. Again in 1870 a similar bill was rejected as "calculated to encourage laziness and make the state of Louisiana a receptacle for the poor of other states." [2] It was not until 1880 that the legisla-

[2] Quoted in Elizabeth Wisner, *Public Welfare Administration in Louisiana* (Chicago: University of Chicago Press, 1930), 29.

ture was willing to make it obligatory that the parishes (counties) support their poor and infirm. The police jurors (county commissioners) were made responsible, along with their many other duties, for granting aid. There is no reference in the act to a special official such as the overseer of the poor. It is of some interest, in view of the previous fear that Louisiana would become a haven for the destitute of other states, that no settlement or residence requirement was provided. Likewise there was no family responsibility clause in the act. Poor farms or almshouses were to be leased or purchased by the police jurors with the proviso that they would be wholly or partially self-supporting—an impossible provision in view of the condition of many of the destitute needing care. As late as 1923 only six of the sixty-four parishes were reported as having poor farms or almshouses, and according to the state Board of Charities and Corrections only six of the parishes appropriated funds for outdoor relief; other parishes may have helped some of the destitute but did not budget separately for this purpose.

In contrast to Louisiana, the basic poor laws of two nearby states, Mississippi and Alabama, with many similar social problems date back to 1807, when both were still territories. The subsequent legislation in the two states is very similar and was apparently influenced by provisions for the poor in the older colonies, especially Virginia, North Carolina, and Georgia, from which many of the older settlers migrated. The legislation is more fully developed than the simple Louisiana act. There were provisions for the appointment of overseers of the poor by the justices of the county courts in each captain's district. Difficulty in persuading inhabitants to accept such appointments is reflected in the provision for a penalty of fifty dollars for refusal to serve, unless excused for age or infirmity. The settlement laws in both states, which required a residence of only six months in a county for public aid eligibility, continued down through the years and were the least stringent requirement imposed in the states. There was also the usual provision for the removal of a person without settlement back to the county where he was thought to belong. The responsibility of members of the family to support a destitute relative, if they were able, was included, thus rounding out the basic conditions of the old poor laws.

Arkansas, originally a part of the Missouri Territory, admitted to the Union in 1836 as the twenty-fifth state, enacted a "pauper" law that same year. This legislation was presumably a reaffirmation of territorial practice that each county provide for its own poor. The state was very much a frontier, with a sparse population living under crude conditions. Two years later, parents and grandparents of sufficient ability were made responsible for the support of their descendants, but no residence requirement was included. Because of the small, scattered population the attitude toward transients and nonresidents was less rigid than in many states. For example, a section of the original act, in contrast to most poor laws, provided that *any* nonresident who fell sick or died and who was without funds or property to pay for his board, nursing, medical care, or burial, was to be given an allowance by the county to meet such contingencies. However, later legislation limited such care to those found to be "paupers." The state supreme court was more specific in deciding that a county was not responsible for burying a poor person unless he had been legally adjudicated a pauper.[3]

Poverty is of course a relative term and today's definition of "the poor" is very broad indeed compared to that embodied in the poor laws. This question of definition was the subject of considerable litigation in many states. One decision rendered by the Arkansas Supreme Court in 1875 stated, "In a general sense, all poor persons may be said to be paupers, but not in the statute meaning of the term. A pauper is defined to be a poor person, particularly one so indigent, so infirm, sick, or disabled as to become an object of public care and support and first be passed upon by some public tribunal. . . . In order to charge the county with the support and maintenance of destitute persons they must first be adjudged paupers by the county courts." [4] Thus an attempt was made to draw a line between the poor person and the pauper, or one legally found destitute of most or all financial resources, and who in some states was required to take the pauper oath.

The vast area of Texas—with 254 counties and about equal in size to the six New England states plus New

[3] *Clark County* v. *Huie,* 49 Ark. 145 (1887).
[4] *Lee County* v. *Lackie,* 30 Ark. 764 (1875).

York, New Jersey, Delaware, Pennsylvania, Ohio, and
Illinois—was obviously far removed from the older colonies in time and experience. Once a part of Mexico, later
an independent republic, and annexed to the United States
in 1845, the state maintained its frontier tradition of mutual aid long after the passage of a poor law the following
year. The statute was silent as to family or relative responsibility, and as for settlement, the act merely said that the
poor person must be a resident of the county and be
eligible for relief; it left the county courts free to de-
termine eligibility. The state needed settlers and the doors
were wide open for immigrants, who began to arrive in
large numbers from abroad as well as from other states.
Later the immigration bureau was active in informing the
world of the unlimited resources and beneficial climate of
Texas, thus attracting not only hardy settlers but also
many ill persons, particularly the tuberculous, seeking a
cure. The western part of the state was considered especially conducive to recovery from tuberculosis, and many
residents and out-of-state persons moved there, often
without sufficient funds to support themselves. Although
the statutes had never provided for the removal of destitute persons from one county to their former place of residence, in 1909 the legislature authorized the state health
officer to isolate and return to their homes "indigent
consumptives" who had settled in counties other than
their own, stating that they soon became charges on
charity, "creating demands on the humanitarianism and
benevolence of such people far beyond their ability to

meet all such requests." [5] Two years later, the legislature noted that so many paupers were being sent into Texas from other states (presumably for health reasons) that an emergency had been created. An act, therefore, provided for six months' residence in a county and one year's residence in the state before the county commissioners could grant public aid.

Florida, another large area, once a Spanish possession, was for a very long time undeveloped and thinly populated. It was admitted to the Union in 1845. What very early provisions there were for the poor is not clear, but in 1868 the constitution stated that the counties should provide for those aged and infirm persons who had a claim on the aid and sympathy of society. Two years later the governor in a message to the legislature complained about the large number of whites and Negroes who drew supplies from the boards of supervisors; he recommended that each county establish an almshouse.

In any consideration of poor law administration in the various states the sundry deterrents imposed on persons seeking aid must be emphasized if we are to understand the problems of the poor. The term *need* was not and could not be satisfactorily defined in the law. Relief recipients in most instances had to be destitute of the necessaries of life, and in determining their need local officials exercised wide discretionary powers. On the other

[5] Quoted in Helen Evans, "Provisions for Public Relief in Texas, 1841–1937" (M. S. thesis, Tulane University School of Social Work, 1941), 21.

hand, where settlement regulations existed, these were specified in the statutes and were mandatory on a state-wide basis. Here we find that the Southern laws were in great contrast to those in the New England states with their lengthy residence requirements, reaching a maximum of ten years in Massachusetts by 1794. The three-year provision in the South Carolina legislation was the longest imposed; North Carolina, Virginia, and Texas each had a one-year requirement; and Alabama and Mississippi retained the original six months' residence clause of the 1807 territorial acts. In the other states there were no definite settlement restrictions, although some states assumed an "intent to settle" for relief recipients who had one year of residence.

Fortunately the old "warning-out" clauses in the early legislation of several Northern states, which militated against the poor in their attempts to move about seeking jobs or to better themselves, were almost wholly absent in the Southern legislation. These measures were designed to prevent persons from acquiring a settlement and to keep them in the status of nonresidents. Through this device, if local officials thought any newcomers were "likely to become dependent" at some future time, they could issue a warning-out notice to depart the town or county. No matter how long such persons remained, they could not gain a settlement, and should they need relief at some future time, the overseers could legally remove them to a locality where they presumably belonged.

Extensive litigation was a prominent feature of poor

law administration in New England and New York. The extremely complex settlement and removal laws, of which residence was only one feature, encouraged costly suits between the towns and counties in their attempts to avoid the burden of relief, and hundreds of controversies reached the higher courts for judicial determination. In comparison, few such controversies are to be found in the court records of the Southern states. The difference in the settlement requirements between the two regions does not reflect a more tolerant attitude in the South toward helping the poor. The explanation probably lies in the pioneer conditions which so long prevailed and the fact that in a largely rural economy little relief was available and there was little public interest in such questions. Moreover, the need for additional inhabitants in the more sparsely settled states may have influenced the legislators in dealing with social welfare.

Provisions obligating certain members of a family, if able, to support destitute relatives were to be found in fewer than half of the Southern poor laws. Denial of the right to vote to recipients of public aid was a common feature of many poor laws. South Carolina, Virginia, and Texas disfranchised such persons, and Louisiana denied the vote to inmates of charitable institutions. A surprising feature of the early Virginia, Alabama, and Mississippi laws was the right to appeal to the county courts when relief was denied by local officials. The Virginia records indicate that the minor courts, in some instances, overruled the overseers of the poor and ordered that relief be

granted. An early Alabama act authorized any poor person who supposed that he was legally entitled to relief
benefits and who was denied assistance by the overseers,
to apply to the county court or any two justices when the
court was in recess. The justices, at their discretion, could
direct the overseers to grant assistance. A state supreme
court decision of 1880 overruled this right of appeal,
stating that the county commissioners were the sole judges
over the administration of public aid, as they were
"clothed with large discretion in the exercise of their
powers". [6] That same year, a Mississippi statute practically nullified the early provision for appeal in that state.

Because many of the poorer rural counties had a higher
proportion of needy inhabitants and less money to spend
on relief than the more prosperous counties, treatment of
the poor was unequal throughout the various states. In
summary, all the states discussed in this chapter followed
the general trend in the United States, enacting legislation
making it mandatory upon the local governmental units
to support their destitute inhabitants from local tax funds.
There were minor differences in the legislation of the
various states, but in the long run these were not significant. The real question remained as to whether mandatory
legislation did, in fact, provide for the poor in many
jurisdictions.

[6] *Henry* v. *Cohen*, 66 Ala. 382 (1880).

III
Local Relief Practices

IT IS ONE thing to say that legislation was passed making it mandatory on local governments throughout the South to support and look after their poor; it is quite another matter to suppose that such laws adequately served the destitute. It would be hazardous to generalize about the relief methods of so many different states over so long a period of time. Social conditions in Virginia, the oldest and most politically mature of the colonies, and in Charleston, South Carolina, which very early was intellectually and culturally advanced for the time, differed from those in settlements with scattered populations living under crude pioneer conditions. For that reason the few illustrations given here, which have been selected from many sources, merely represent some of the ways the poor were dealt with; they in no sense provide a total picture of local Southern relief practices.

For instance, early Virginia records indicate that a considerable proportion of the tax dollar was spent on outdoor relief in some parishes, while in other parishes the poor were grossly neglected. The tithe, or tax, was usually paid in tobacco (sometimes in wheat or maize), and in the decade 1720–30 Bristol Parish levied a tax amounting to 370,982 pounds of tobacco on the local inhabitants. Of this amount 34,415 pounds, or about 9 percent of the total cost of parish expenditures, was spent on relief. In 1744 St. Peter's Parish aided thirteen persons at a cost of 7,040 pounds of tobacco—over 15 percent of the total levy for that year. The same parish kept Widow Faulkner for twenty years at a cost of 20,619 pounds of tobacco. Relief recipients usually boarded in the homes of local inhabitants at the expense of the parish and received permanent care if old or disabled. There were occasional proposals that all the poor in a parish be "farmed out" or auctioned off to the lowest bidder who would contract to care for them at a cost agreed upon by the church wardens, but there is no evidence that such plans were carried out.

Most of the New England towns had a special official, the overseer of the poor, to look after the poor and administer relief. By contrast, the parish vestries and church wardens in the Southern colonies had many other duties. As the governing body of the parishes, the vestries levied and collected the tithes, appointed clergymen, investigated cases of immorality and disorder, and administered relief and apprenticeship laws. As the population increased and moved westward, new parishes were created. Failure of the vestry system of relief in these areas led to numerous complaints that the destitute suffered from want of proper support, and the Virginia General Assembly in a series of acts dissolved the vestries and ordered the sheriffs to elect overseers of the poor. Finally, in 1785, a general act provided for such officials in all counties; thus the care of the poor in Virginia passed from the control of the Anglican Church to that of the civil authorities.

In North Carolina, indifference to the needs of the poor did not cease with the disestablishment of the church. Many counties continued to ignore the poor law, failing to appoint overseers of the poor. Even when elected, some persons failed to qualify for this post. In consequence, a penalty of ten pounds for failure to serve was imposed. Inhabitants in need of relief must have been numerous, for the same legislation refers to the situation of the destitute as a scandal and disgrace to society. In contrast to this recognition of the extent of poverty, in some of the colonies so little cash relief was administered that "pauperism" was regarded as practically nonexistent. Governor George R. Gilmer of Georgia, speaking in 1830, undoubtedly expressed the opinion of a majority of the group in power when he said, "We have no such class as the poor. Our lands are so cheap, and the absolute necessaries of life so easily obtained that the number of dependent poor are scarcely sufficient to give exercise to the virtues of charity in individuals. A beggar is almost as rare with us as a prince. Children instead of being an incumbrance to the poor of our country, are their riches." [1]

When a subsistence standard of living was the lot of many, there was inevitably little concern over the ques-

[1] Quoted in Myldred F. Hutchins, "The History of Poor Law Legislation in Georgia, 1733–1919" (M.S. thesis, Tulane University School of Social Work, 1940), 66.

tion of poverty. Moreover, the social structure of the
South, both before and after the Civil War, must be considered in any reference to the attitudes towards the poor
and lowly. About one-third of the population were Negro
slaves who were the responsibility of their masters and
therefore not considered eligible for public aid. As time
went on, there were also the free Negroes or manumitted
slaves; fear that they might become a danger to the body
politic led to certain restrictions on their freedom. It has
been suggested that such measures were also considered
necessary to protect the public against being charged for
their maintenance. For instance, in an early North Carolina law (1777) the state asserted its control over emancipation by providing that the county courts must approve
petitions for freedom, whereas formerly a master could
free a slave without court action.[2] Likewise in Tennessee,
and perhaps in other Southern states, opposition to the
freeing of slaves grew as the manumission societies became
active. Tennessee legislation in 1831 provided that no slave
could be emancipated except on condition of his removal
from the state. There is no way of knowing how many
free Negroes—if any—were helped through the poor
laws, either by outdoor relief or in the almshouses, but it is
clear that emancipation did little to improve their social or
economic situation. A substantial proportion of the non-
slaveholding class, those at the bottom of the heap, were
the "poor whites," as they were generally labeled by more

[2] *Acts of North Carolina*, 1777, Chap. 6, Sec. 2.

fortunate citizens. Various terms, sometimes of contempt, were commonly used in different states to designate this group: "poor white trash," "tarheels," "crackers," "red necks," "hillbillies," and "Cajuns" (the South Louisiana inhabitants of French-Canadian origin). Many were illiterate and subject to malaria and hookworm. They lived on farms or small patches of poor land, and it was assumed that food and fuel were close at hand. They were poor in contrast to the yeoman farmers and the plantation owners but usually had enough to eat, though the diet might be deficient. The climate was less rugged than in the North and they somehow managed a subsistence standard of living which often left them indifferent to their miserable plight. Set apart as they were from the dominant groups who held political power, they and their situation were largely ignored.

Relief grants, when available, in Southern counties were generally mere doles or relief in kind. It is impossible to know from the scanty records whether they were supplementary to other resources or were the sole funds available to applicants. It is also impossible to judge the adequacy of cash payments in terms of local standards of living or the value of the dollar over the years. An early court record of Bradley County, Arkansas, is typical of many poor law records: "Come Abadiah Walker and shows the Court that he is a citizen of this county and that he is to all intensions and purposes a pauper and prays the Court for an appropriation. Thereupon the Court grants said prayer and orders that the sum of $12 be appropriated to said pauper for the term." [3] In 1880, after the passage of the first poor law, the police jurors of Jefferson Parish, Louisiana, fixed a rate of twenty-five cents per diem and "no more" for the maintenance of a pauper. To avoid cash payments, in some instances widows with children and the infirm who were destitute were granted free licenses (for a limited period) to run small stores or to peddle goods.

The practice of "auctioning off" the poor in some public place to the lowest bidder, singly or in "lots," was widely followed in New England before the Civil War. There was considerable criticism of this method of abrogating a public responsibility to private citizens whose main motive on bidding to care for all the poor of a town or county must have been to make a profit out of the transaction. Fortunately, this arrangement does not appear to have been common in the Southern states, although there are a few available records of the practice here and there. Some of the early North Carolina documents record the use of this method of care, but in 1876 the state legislature passed an act forbidding the letting out of paupers at public auction and specified that they must be supported by friends or other persons when not maintained at the county home. But as late as 1897 the commissioners of Baxter County, a rural mountainous section of northern Arkansas, callously ordered the sheriff

[3] Quoted in Bernice Greaves Ratcliffe, "100 Years of Poor Relief Administration in Arkansas, 1836–1936" (M.S. thesis, Tulane University School of Social Work, 1947), 37.

to collect all the paupers who were scattered over the county and to contract for their care to the lowest bidder.

In the foregoing description of the Southern poor laws many technical aspects of the legislation have been omitted. One that was of importance in some states was the right of a third party, a citizen in the community, to recover the cost of aiding a poor person when such care was urgently needed. At a time when public relief was not well organized or was nonexistent there were, of course, instances when such aid was rendered by sympathetic local citizens. The Mississippi code of 1880 for example, reinforcing earlier legislation, clearly specified that applications for reimbursement from parties who had fed, clothed, and administered to a pauper (one who could not be removed to the almshouse) were valid claims against the local poor law officials. But counties did not always honor such claims and several suits were carried to the circuit courts and on to the Mississippi Supreme Court in attempts to secure reimbursement.

Generally speaking, in litigation over public aid, local officials sought out every technicality in the law to avoid paying the costs of relief. The reasoning over such technicalities often seems tortuous to the layman. This is especially true in a suit before the Mississippi Supreme Court in 1898. A Dr. Harrison had sued Tallahatchie County in the circuit court and recovered $96 for emergency medical services rendered to a Mr. Simmons. The court apparently based its favorable decision on the evidence that Dr. Harrison had called on a Dr. High, who as a member of the board of supervisors decided that the man was a pauper and would die if not treated. He requested Dr. Harrison to care for Simmons and promised that he would see that the board of supervisors paid the bill. However, the case was carried to the higher court and the judges accepted evidence that Simmons was indigent, had a blind wife and several minor children unable to support their parents, and that he was urgently in need of medical treatment. But they took refuge in a clause in the 1892 code providing that a poor person must be formally adjudicated a pauper and presumably must take the pauper's oath. Since there was no record that Simmons had ever been declared a pauper by the *entire* board of supervisors, the judgment of the lower court was reversed and the case remanded for a new trial.[4] Fortunately, the patient had recovered and could leave the legal battle over his case to others.

ALMSHOUSE CARE

Gradually over the decades the poor farm or almshouse system of care became the main resource for the destitute, which frequently included the aged, the disabled, the insane and feebleminded, mothers with children, and able-bodied men down on their luck (along with their families). In some counties, outdoor relief or cash grants to some persons in need were continued along with in-

[4] *Board of Supervisors of Tallahatchie County* v. *T. B. Harrison,* 75 Miss. 744 (1898).

stitutional care, but in others the poor farm appears to have been the only resource for the destitute. The American almshouse has frequently been indicted as a social institution. One of the more dramatic criticisms of this type of care is found in a study of the system made in the 1920's: "The word 'poorhouse' has become the threatening symbol of one of humanity's greatest degradations. To many a despairing heart it comes with a sound like the crack of doom. It is a word of hate and loathing, for it includes the composite horrors of poverty, disgrace, loneliness, humiliation, abandonment and degradation." [5] Perhaps not all the poor assigned to such institutions felt quite as degraded as this quotation indicates, but obviously in a region so largely rural in character, where many families had a meager living, the Southern poor farm was too often a wretched shelter for the destitute. In some counties, the poor farm was let out by contract to the lowest bidder, who in a sense bought the labor of the poor (in view of the condition of the inmates it must have been inefficient). Therefore, he could not, in most instances, make a profit or a living for himself except by gross neglect of his charges. In other counties, the almshouse or poor farm was built on the same grounds as the convict camps. The paupers placed at one time on the convict farms of eight Mississippi counties were said to be far more comfortable than if they had been relegated to a poor farm. The food and maintenance of the buildings

[5] Harry C. Evans, *The American Poor Farm and Its Inmates* (Des Moines, Iowa: Loyal Order of Moose, 1926), epigraph.

were better and general living conditions more agreeable. In fact, in many counties, although not all, there was only a fine line drawn between the pauper and the offender against the law.

The regulations governing an Alabama poor farm provide some insight into the daily lives of the inmates. These regulations were adopted in 1885 by the Jefferson County (Birmingham) court of commissioners. Each pauper was to put on clean clothes once a week, and a special day was designated when they must wash their clothes. On another day of the week they were directed to sun their bedding and scour their rooms. All bedding was to be washed and boiled once a month, when new straw would be put in their beds. As for work assignments, the keeper of the poor farm was to choose certain paupers to do the cooking for all the inmates; and all paupers were regularly to perform such work as they were able, as determined by an inspector who came once a week to check up on the management. No pauper was to be allowed to leave the premises of the institution without the permission of the keeper; and finally, any pauper failing to comply with the regulations was subject to the penalty of having his rations reduced, or was otherwise punished in ways determined by the inspector.

In many Southern counties the number of inmates given shelter in the local almshouse or poor farm was so small that the cost of adequate care to meet individual needs would have seemed prohibitive. The poor house of McIntosh County, Georgia, is representative of many. In

1893 there were only six inmates; a year later the number had dropped to three. For twenty-six years the matron had been paid a monthly wage of ten dollars and the assistant five dollars. The personnel put in charge of the county poor farms indicates the type of care furnished. According to a study of the Tennessee institutions, as late as 1938 the superintendent was still referred to as the "keeper of the poor" and was the successful low bidder for the job. Usually he was a farmer—and not a very successful one—who had some political influence in securing the bid. In one county the keeper was sixty-three years old; his wife, who did the cooking without a salary, was sixty. The bid was eight dollars per capita per month for the twenty-three inmates. In another county a young couple with two small children were the keepers. Again the wife did the cooking and the nursing but neither she nor her husband received a salary. Fifty cents a day was allowed for the bed-ridden and twenty cents per diem for the other inmates, together with the privilege of farming thirty-nine acres of poor land.

The principle of local responsibility, with the use of local tax funds to support the poor, was probably inevitable in the early period. This system continued until the 1930's, when federal funds poured in under the Federal Emergency Relief Administration, the Works Progress Administration, and shortly afterwards the Social Security Administration. Local administration of the poor laws, however, had been generally inefficient and often corrupted by politicalization and petty graft. The dispensers of relief, the county commissioners, the justices of the peace, the wardens of the poor, the overseers, and other elected officials were ill equipped to deal with problems presented by applicants for public aid, and they usually dealt with the destitute in a perfunctory manner.

Again, the records of the court of county commissioners of Jefferson County, Alabama, during the latter years of the nineteenth century provide an illustration, and a fairly typical one, of local administration. The commissioners met often and much time was spent considering burial expenses of paupers and the purchase of coffins. Bills for the maintenance of the poor farm were examined item by item, as there was no fixed budget for its upkeep, and few meetings were held when "charity orders" were not approved for some applicant. Notations of such sums as three dollars a month to a widow for support of her blind daughter, ten dollars a month to a couple, and five dollars a month to a W. Short for the support of a pauper frequently appear in the records of the commissioners. These orders were the first cash relief given in this county and as there was no supervision of such cases, payments often continued year after year, or until a coffin was ordered for the pauper. Evidently, the issuance of cash relief became a nuisance, and in 1897 the commissioners unanimously ordered it discontinued and all paupers sent to the poor farm. An exception was made with respect to minor children, who were to be supported in a private institution, the Mercy Home, on a subsidy basis. Thus we see the swing to almshouse care with practically no outdoor relief available until 1932, when federal emergency relief for the unemployed was instituted.

Any attempt to pass judgment on the treatment of the destitute in the Southern region, at this late date, is futile except to say that it was characterized by the same inefficiency and inhumanity that generally governed the poor law. As Edith Abbott has said, "A nation's standard of living determines its standard of eligibility for public aid." [6] This is true not only of provisions made for the relief of the poor over the nation as a whole, but of the states and local communities. Over much of the rural South living standards were exceedingly low and the structure of society far from democratic. Today it is evident that an economic and political revolution was necessary before substantial changes in help for the destitute and lowly would occur.

RELIEF DURING THE CIVIL WAR

Reference should be made to the new and unprecedented relief problems created by the Civil War. As in the Northern states, the war inspired widespread charitable activities on the part of Southern women, who held innumerable balls, fairs, bazaars, and other money-raising benefits to aid members of the armed forces and their families. No comprehensive account will be offered here of the various provisions for dependents of Confederate

[6] Edith Abbott, *Public Assistance*, 12.

soldiers at the local and state levels of government. A few illustrations will suggest the concern expressed for these families, many of whom were poor in contrast to other segments of the population but had managed to get along without public aid before the war. The poor laws were presumably available to support those in need but they carried so much stigma that it was unthinkable that the wives and children of the brave fighting forces should have to accept the indignities of pauper relief. As early as 1861 the governor of Alabama, in a message to a special session of the legislature, called attention to the condition of the many families among the poorer classes and predicted that there would be much suffering and perhaps starvation as the war continued. He urged that the county commissioners be empowered to levy and collect a special tax for the purpose of raising funds to purchase food for those without support. The governor went further to state that if such a tax could not be collected, then public property in the counties should be pledged as money borrowed to meet the dire needs of the poor.

In 1863, eight separate acts were passed by the Mississippi legislature, a few of them for the benefit of disabled soldiers but the majority for the relief of families. One was for the relief of persons made destitute by the seizure and destruction of their property; another, to provide indigent families with meal, salt, and other staples. In 1864 the governor of Mississippi, anticipating the defeat of the Confederate armies, in a message to the legislature predicted widespread poverty. He recognized that the Confederate government would have no funds to aid the states and proposed that the six million acres of public domain in Mississippi be reserved to provide homesteads for soldiers and their families as a gesture for their loyal service to the Confederate cause. Again the following year, the governor spoke of the great amount of destitution and reported that during the previous year 139,042 white families, out of a total population of 525,000, had been supplied with salt and meal. He estimated that a quarter of a million persons would have to be furnished food until they could raise it for themselves. The legislature empowered him to issue bonds for the relief of the destitute. Thereafter the burden of disbursing temporary relief was largely borne by the federal government through the Freedmen's Bureau.

Accounts of two relief efforts at the local levels, one in Georgia and the other in Louisiana, afford typical illustrations of the ways in which a segment of the population was helped. The records of Dougherty County, Georgia, indicate the method followed in a black-belt county of the state. This was a new county created by legislative act 120 years after the founding of the state, with the town of Albany as the county seat. The white population largely comprised small farmers and a middle-class economic element; unlike many Georgia counties, Dougherty did not have a predominance of large landowning and well-to-do groups. In 1860, out of a total population of 8,295, fully 75 percent were Negro. The ratio of Negro to white inhabitants was even higher down through 1910.

Poor relief was administered by the justices of the peace, and over the period from 1855 to 1862, only seven paupers received aid either through small doles or relief in kind. The Civil War brought a new experience in social welfare to the people of the county, unaccustomed as they were to providing for the poor. Many white families were without support as the husbands and fathers left to fight in the Confederate forces.

Patriotism ran high in the early days of the conflict; and in 1861 the Dougherty County officials, on recommendation of the grand jury, prepared to provide relief to families of soldiers out of local funds. A committee of five citizens was appointed and was given supervision over the program. In order to finance the cost, the local treasurer was ordered to issue scrip redeemable with interest in six months. A military fund was created and food supplies were purchased and distributed to those in need. Despite the naïve anticipations of many Southerners, there was no quick victory for the Confederate forces, and as the months and years wore on, poverty increased and disabled soldiers began to drift back to the county. By 1863 it was necessary for the state government to come to the aid of the counties with funds for an increased distribution of food. A few months before Georgia surrendered to the Union army, the chairman of the Albany relief committee submitted a memorial to the inferior court showing that 350 to 400 persons had received 2,000 pounds of bacon and 250 bushels of wheat monthly during the war. For two years thereafter, the state continued to provide corn for destitute veterans and their families. There is no mention of the payment of Confederate pensions for the next twenty-eight years, when a few disabled and dependent veterans and widows are listed as recommended for such state allowances.

The records of St. Landry Parish, Louisiana, provide a different picture of Civil War relief methods. This was an old, settled, and relatively prosperous community where destitute persons had been aided from the parish treasury long before the statewide poor law was passed in 1880, and such relief was continued throughout the war. But for the new poor, namely the families of Confederate soldiers left behind without support, a special fund was created in 1862 from which cash grants were made to such dependents. By January of the next year the state legislature acted to provide payments for dependents of officers and noncommissioned personnel of the military and naval forces who were unable to support themselves. St. Landry Parish also distributed such staples as corn, rice, and salt, and issued wool and cotton cards, but never relied entirely on such provisions to support the wives and children of the fighting forces.

In contrast to the relatively lavish benefits provided for the families of the Northern forces, all resources of relief for soldiers' families in the Confederate states were meager indeed. One student of the period states that governmental benefits and charitable gifts for members of the Northern armed forces, their dependents, and other war sufferers were unprecedented. It is estimated that the federal, state, and local governments spent $600 million on enlistment bounties and that an additional $100 million was raised from private sources for this purpose. Much of the cash was turned over to needy relatives and was in substance a form of family relief. Furthermore, veterans of the defeated Confederate forces and their dependents were, of course, not eligible for federal benefits after the war; this burden had to be carried by the states. In contrast, as early as 1861, $1 million dollars was being paid in pensions to some eight thousand members of the Union forces, and by 1907 pension payments had increased to just under $140 million.[7] The circulation of such large sums (for that period) inevitably contributed to the general prosperity in the North during and following the war. Moreover, the older established charities appear not to have suffered financially because of the war, and the experience of voluntary giving so widely stimulated during this period continued thereafter.

[7] Emerson David Fitz, *Social and Industrial Conditions in the North during the Civil War* (New York: Macmillan Co., 1910), Chap. 11.

IV
Early Care of the Mentally Ill

ALTHOUGH THERE is no way of knowing the extent of mental illness in any of the colonies during the colonial period, it is evident from scattered references that the restraint and care of such persons became a troublesome problem. The first attempt in America to provide hospital facilities for such persons was the Pennsylvania Hospital in Philadelphia, established by the provincial legislature in 1751. Although other ill persons were to be admitted, the insane (or "lunatics," as they were called) had attracted much public concern. A petition to the House of Representatives stated that persons distempered in mind and deprived of their rational facilities had greatly increased; some were so violent they were a terror to their neighbors; others wasted their substance, depriving themselves of support; while not a few were the prey of unscrupulous persons. Paying patients were to be admitted to the hospital, but the need to care for those unable to pay is evident in all the reports. Benjamin Franklin, Philadelphia's most distinguished citizen, was a leader in urging the establishment of this facility and became a member of the first board of managers. From the beginning the Pennsylvania Hospital was a teaching center. Dr. Benjamin

Rush, a signer of the Declaration of Independence and an outstanding philanthropist who treated the mentally ill in this hospital, is referred to as the "father of American psychiatry." His treatise *Inquiries and Observations upon the Diseases of the Mind* (1812) was the first volume on mental illness published in this country.

A few illustrations can be given of attempts in the Southern states to provide for the insane. In North Carolina, during the latter part of the eighteenth century, the first almshouses established by an act of the legislature (in seven counties) were for the care of such patients, and the church wardens were directed to keep them confined as long as necessary. Another illustration of a local provision, and a quite different one, is to be found in the New Orleans police code of 1808, which provided that "furious madmen" found on the streets were the responsibility of the nearest relative on penalty of being answerable for any trouble such persons would cause; or if there were no relatives, they were to be put in some secure place at the cost of the city. Since there was no almshouse in existence at this time, presumably the more violent individuals were placed in the local jail and the less harmful ones allowed to roam the streets. With the rise of state hospitals for the mentally ill before the Civil War, there was some slight improvement in the care of such patients confined in county jails and almshouses.

To Virginia goes credit for founding, in 1769, the first state hospital solely for the treatment of such patients in this country. In view of the protracted efforts to find effective treatment for the mentally disturbed, the short preamble to the act passed by the House of Burgesses is of interest today. It indicates the intention of the legislators that this new institution was to provide treatment and *cure* for those mental patients able to be helped. The act stated in part, "Whereas, Several persons of insane and disordered minds have been frequently found wandering in different parts of this colony and no certain provision having been yet made either towards effecting a cure for those who are not become quite desperate, nor retaining others who may be dangerous to society . . . "[1] The institution was named The Public Hospital for Persons of Insane and Disordered Minds.

The trustees, who were to establish and oversee the administration of the hospital, were named in the act and bore such prominent Virginia names as Blair, Carter, Randolph, and Wythe. The hospital, which was located in Williamsburg, was later called the Eastern State Hospital. It served as the only facility for the mentally ill until the Western State Hospital in Staunton was built, about sixty years later. The success of the Williamsburg hospital was considered to have influenced the building of the second state hospital in the United States, which was located in Lexington, Kentucky, in 1824 and also the South Carolina state facility for the mentally ill in Columbia in 1828. The names of two men who in their twenties served as superintendents of the Virginia institutions should be

[1] Sophonisba P. Breckinridge, *Public Welfare Administration in the United States,* 73–76.

mentioned. They were Dr. John W. Galt, head of the Williamsburg asylum, and Dr. Francis T. Stribling, head of the Staunton hospital. Both were in the forefront of the movement for hospital care of the mentally ill, and in 1844 they were among the thirteen doctors who founded the Association of Medical Superintendents of American Institutions for the Insane, now the American Psychiatric Association. Dr. Galt, a native of Virginia, although young, was regarded as the most scholarly of the group and took first place as a writer and interpreter of mental illness. Unfortunately, in later years many of the heads of the state institutions were dubious political appointees and the standard of care of the patients often declined in many states.

What was done about the disturbed slave or free Negro cannot be fully stated, although there are occasional references to these groups in the population. A curious clause in the 1751 South Carolina poor law provided subsistence for lunatic slaves belonging to persons *too poor* to care for them. The justice of the peace and the overseer of the poor were required to prevent such slaves from "doing mischief" by securing them in some safe, convenient place in the parish, with the expense of their care to be borne by the local treasury. As it was not uncommon at this time to keep mentally ill persons in cages and to incarcerate them under cruel conditions, the fate of the South Carolina slaves may not have been any worse. It was almost a hundred years before the legislature authorized the admission of Negroes into the state hospital, which had opened in 1828.

The Virginia policy regarding care of Negroes is somewhat confusing. One of the earliest patients admitted to the Williamsburg hospital was a free mulatto woman named Charity, and many years later the legislature made legal the admission of insane slaves to this institution when suitable space was available, after all white persons had been accommodated. In the beginning the Staunton hospital made no distinction as to race, but twenty years later the policy changed. A report stated that owing to the construction of the buildings it was not practical to provide suitable provisions for Negro patients, and moreover it was inexpedient to house the two races in the same institution. The legislature than appropriaed funds to provide free care for the Negroes at Williamsburg. The scant records referring to the care of the Negroes often mention "persons of color," a term which probably applied to mulattoes and free Negroes and not to the slaves, whose masters were expected to care for them on the plantations. In any event, we have no way of knowing the extent of mental illness among Negroes, slave or free, at this time.

Dorothea Lynde Dix of Boston invaded the Southern states before the Civil War, when there was already tension over the slavery issue. Her work in the South is an important chapter in the career of this remarkable woman. Here was a Yankee and a woman, traveling alone at a time when Southern women did not undertake such missions and when journeys back and forth across the region were extremely arduous. She traveled by trains, stagecoaches, and lumber wagons over muddy roads and across swollen streams, and often found herself in the malaria-stricken areas of the South. Indefatigable in her inspection of jails, almshouses, and the few facilities caring for the mentally ill, she was well prepared for her work with the legislatures of the several states.

Her visits in the 1840's and again in 1859–60 took her to every Confederate state, with the possible exception of Florida. After the war, she returned in 1869, 1870, and 1871 (and then included Florida in her itinerary). Beginning in 1846, she traveled by steamboat from Louisville to New Orleans. After a visit to Charity Hospital, where separate apartments to house the insane had been built in 1820, she wrote; "I have seen incomparably more to approve than to censure in New Orleans." [2] A separate state hospital in Jackson, Louisiana, was authorized by the legislature a year later, and she returned to visit this institution in 1860.

Her reception in Southern legislative halls bears testimony to her great gifts as a lobbyist. North Carolina was the only one of the original thirteen colonies without state care for the mentally ill, and Miss Dix in her forthright manner set about to correct this situation. As always

[2] Quoted in Helen E. Marshall, *Dorothea Dix* (Chapel Hill: University of North Carolina Press, 1937), 112. See also 113–23, 192–98.

when lobbying in a new state, she came to the capital well prepared. She had spent three months visiting jails and almshouses throughout the state gathering facts about the condition of the insane, the epileptics, and the mentally retarded. It had been the policy of North Carolina to send a few patients to institutions in neighboring states, while others remained in the homes of relatives, but the majority were to be found in the cells of county jails and the cages of almshouses. Miss Dix included these facts in her memorial to the legislature. She achieved her first and most dramatic success in the South when, following her impassioned appeal, $100,000 was appropriated to build a hospital, the first for the mentally ill provided by North Carolina.

She had a keen sense of political strategy. A brief account of her methods in North Carolina will serve to illustrate the procedures she used in other states. She had learned that the Democrats, who had lately come to power in the legislature, were considered conservative about appropriating funds for new projects because of their interest in a railroad for the western counties. Undaunted, she summoned some of the leading Democrats to confer with her in Mansion House, where she had established headquarters. Miss Dix's reputation as a lobbyist had undoubtedly preceded her visit to North Carolina, and the legislators responded to her invitation. As it happened, James Dobbin, a leading member of the Democratic Party, lived with his wife in Mansion House during the sessions of the legislature. He agreed to see the $100,000 appropriation for the new hospital through both houses of the legislature. Mrs. Dobbin had been very ill and was nursed by Miss Dix. When Mrs. Dobbin died, Miss Dix accompanied the body to Fayetteville. As it turned out, Mrs. Dobbin on her deathbed had extracted a promise from her husband to support Miss Dix's bill, and so he did. In view of the fact that the total annual revenues of the state were only $200,000—aside from the so-called Literary Fund (probably a school revenue) the willingness of the legislature to find other sources of revenue to finance the new hospital was a tribute to Miss Dix's effectiveness as a speaker for her cause. She was urged to allow the new institution to bear her name and finally agreed that it could be called Dix Hall in honor of her grandfather, Dr. Elijah Dix—the only one of the state institutions she worked to establish to bear the Dix name.

In Tennessee her legislative efforts were crowned with success when an appropriation was passed to provide better facilities than the small stone building which had cared for patients since 1832. She returned to the state in 1860 and was influential in persuading the legislature to construct a second hospital in Knoxville and to build an additional wing on the old one in Nashville.

That same year, learning that the appropriation for the South Carolina hospital was in danger, she promptly left her work in Mississippi and rode three days and nights to reach the state capital, Columbia. Within a month Miss Dix had influenced the passage of a bill appropriating $155,000 for the maintenance of the hospital.

In some of the Southern states Miss Dix visited, there were local citizens and members of the medical societies who had labored with little response to arouse public interest in proper care of the mentally ill. The time was ripe for a forward movement in the state hospital systems. With her extensive knowledge of the subject and her ability to gather and interpret the facts about conditions in the almshouses and jails, Miss Dix provided the necessary outside stimulus to legislative action.

For instance, the local medical society of Selma, Alabama, had made considerable effort to gather information about the costs of state hospitals and to explore a site for a building. The state medical association joined them in an appeal to the legislature, but with no success. During 1849 Miss Dix spent several weeks in Alabama visiting jails and almshouses in preparation for her memorial to the legislature. A brief excerpt from this long document illustrates the special quality of her appeal, which was to characterize all of her appearances before state assemblies:

I do not come to present a view of fancied ills—to rattle the chain, nor to utter the shriek of the maniac in your ear. I do not come to depict in false and too vivid colors before your amazed vision the horrors of . . . the manifestations of insanity as it breaks down with restless force the noblest intellect, overwhelms the judgement, and distorts the affectations by extravagant and fearful delusions. . . . I come in the name of those who cannot plead for themselves to urge of you the Legislators, individually and collectively, such a monied appropriation as shall construct a State Hospital on a basis so liberal and substantial that your fellow-citizens who suffer under the affliction of insanity whether rich or poor may receive within your own borders the means of care and cure.[3]

The memorial included factual information about mental illness and state hospital systems. It was cordially received and referred to a select committee, which urged the passage of the bill to establish a hospital. Two thousand copies of the memorial were ordered printed and there was general optimism that the bill would pass, but suddenly everything was thrown into confusion when the state capitol caught fire. Miss Dix left Alabama feeling that her efforts had been wasted and that there was no prospect of further action, but she had underestimated the effect of her visit. The state medical association appointed a committee to draft a second memorial and three years later influenced passage of a bill to authorize the building of the first state hospital for the mentally ill in Alabama. Unfortunately, due to shortage of funds the hospital did not open until 1860.

Miss Dix's next appeal was to the Mississippi legislature. Despite her fears that she would be unsuccessful in that state, a bill to establish a state hospital was passed, and before she left Jackson an appropriation had been made for the building. Her memorial to the legislature effectively developed the concept of the insane as "wards of

[3] [Dorothea L. Dix], "Memorial Soliciting a State Hospital for the Insane, Submitted to the Legislature of Alabama, November 15, 1849," *Alabama House of Representatives Documents*, No. 2.

the state." [4] Again she was cordially received by the members of the legislature. Various citizens urged that the new hospital be named for her, but she refused.

As she traveled throughout the Confederate states, Miss Dix found cases of neglect and cruelty, hospitals overcrowded and poorly supported, and commitment laws antiquated and impractical. In a memorial to Congress requesting federal aid to the states for the care of the mentally ill, she commented on a few of the Southern states. In Virginia, where the first action was taken to provide state hospital care, there were insufficient resources for the increasing number of patients in the state, and this was to be a constant problem in all states in the Union. In South Carolina, there were deplorable abuses, and the insane were to be found in pens, bound with cords and chains. Georgia appeared to have fewer mentally ill persons than either North or South Carolina, but the dreary cells and jails were much the same. In Tennessee there was the same cruelty and neglect. The number of patients was constantly increasing along with the rising population, and patients were confined in cabins, pens, cells, and dungeons, abandoned to filth and neglect. However, in another connection, she commented that the South taken as a region showed little contrast to other sections of the country she had visited.

After visits to other states, North and South, she fore-

[4] [Dorothea L. Dix], *Memorial Soliciting Adequate Appropriations for the Construction of a State Hospital for the Insane in the State of Mississippi* (Jackson: Mississippi Legislature, 1850).

saw the need for federal aid if sufficient hospital facilities were ever to be available. In 1848 she introduced her famous memorial to Congress. Knowing that Congress had been generous if not lavish in parceling out federal lands for railroad construction and even for private speculation, Miss Dix appealed for five million acres (valued at a dollar an acre) to constitute a fund to be granted to the thirty states on the basis of their populations. The bill was supported by many prominent individuals, and the Association of Medical Superintendents of American Institutions for the Insane yearly passed resolutions supporting the bill, but it failed to pass. Undaunted, Miss Dix spent the next six years in and out of congressional corridors promoting her measure. In 1849 she increased her request to twelve million five hundred acres for the indigent blind, deaf and dumb, and insane, specifying that ten million acres be set aside for the care of the latter group. Finally in 1854 a bill to provide ten million acres in grants to the states passed both houses of Congress, only to be vetoed by President Franklin Pierce.

One cannot leave the subject of Dorothea Dix's efforts in the Southern states without some further consideration of her career as one of the truly great reformers in the social welfare field. Like other eminent leaders, she was unwilling to accept the status quo. She set about mobilizing public opinion in the direction of curative treatment of the mentally ill. Without the help of national committees or organizational support, Miss Dix in a sense was a national movement in herself. A review of the methods she

followed, of fact-gathering, the preparations of memorials and bills, their presentation to legislative bodies, and
the rallying of public opinion is not without value today.
Her first memorial to the Massachusetts legislature, submitted in 1843, was the model for the appeals she presented in other states.[5] She had first spent eighteen months
visiting every almshouse, workhouse, and jail in the state
and was able to document the number and condition of
the indigent insane and feebleminded that were cruelly
neglected and without treatment or proper care. She not
only incorporated the harsh facts in considerable detail in
her memorial but wrote with such moral passion about
the responsibility of the citizens of that state for the sick
and suffering that she moved the legislature to act in providing additional facilities.

There is frequent discussion among social work organizations about the imperative to engage in social action.
Miss Dix's work provides a good illustration of the contrast between the earlier reform movements, in which
individual leadership played a significant role, and group
action and the processes of social action as they are discussed today. Moreover, very few social reformers today
are apt to feel the messianic inspiration that in part motivated Miss Dix, as when she wrote to a friend, "I am the
Hope of the poor crazed beings who pine in cells and
stalls and cages and waste rooms, . . . I am the Revelation
of hundreds of wailing, suffering creatures hidden in your

[5] Dorothea L. Dix, *Memorial to the Legislature of Massachusetts, 1848,* Old South Leaflets, General Series, VI, No. 148.

private dwellings, and in pens, and cabins—shut out, cut off from all healing influence, from all mind restoring cares." [6] Her plea for federal aid anticipated the Mental Health Act of 1947 by nearly one hundred years. This gap in time between Dorothea Dix's insight into the need for federal aid to the states and the 1947 act further illustrates the hard fact that movements towards welfare objectives do not necessarily progress in a straight and upward path.

[6] Quoted in Marshall, *Dorothea Dix*, 115.

V
The Freedmen's Bureau

THE WELL-KNOWN British historian D. W. Brogan,
who is a student of American history, has characterized
the Civil War as a human tragedy on a scale never equaled
before or since in our history, a war in which the country
lost proportionally far more lives than in World War
II. Moreover he views it as a disastrous experience physi-
cally and morally, a prelude to a long period of humiliation and despair, and one of the watersheds in the nation's
history.[1] The devastation created by the wars of this gen-
eration are still so fresh in our minds that it takes little imagination to recapture the conditions prevailing
throughout the Confederacy during the closing days of
hostilities and for many years after the end of the war.
There was, of course, no Marshall Plan to help in the re-
habilitation of the Southern economy, but the relief program of the Freedmen's Bureau, which has been called
our first federal welfare agency, should not be omitted in
a history of Southern social welfare.

Congress passed the bill to establish the Bureau of Ref-

[1] D. W. Brogan, in *A Fresh Appraisal of the Civil War*, ed.
Alfred Kazin (New York: Harcourt, Brace and World, 1961),
140–68.

ugees, Freedmen, and Abandoned Lands in March, 1865, just a month before the surrender of the Confederate forces. This title gives little indication of the scope of the programs or the powers delegated to the bureau. The distribution of relief in kind to the hungry and destitute was an important but short-lived activity of the agency. The management of abandoned and confiscated property and the attempts to adjudicate disputes between Negroes and whites, to put the freedmen to work, and to educate Negro children must be omitted from this discussion, although they probably had a greater impact on the Southern states than the temporary distribution of food and clothing. It has been said, perhaps with some exaggeration, that "no more difficult task can confront the historical investigator than an attempt to form a just estimate of the work, character and general influence of the Freedmen's Bureau." [2]

As in other social legislation passed by Congress, the ideas embodied in the bureau act did not spring full-blown into the minds of the legislators but were the outgrowth of considerable past experience. All during the war, slaves left the plantations to crowd around the army camps wherever the Northern troops advanced. When General Ulysses S. Grant invaded Mississippi in the fall of 1862, for instance, the Negroes flocked to his camp in droves; after the fall of Vicksburg the next year, some fifty thou-

[2] Quoted in George R. Bentley, *A History of the Freedmen's Bureau* (Philadelphia: University of Pennsylvania Press, 1955), vii.

sand helpless, illiterate slaves swarmed along the banks of the Mississippi River waiting to be fed and protected. At the end of the conflict there were tens of thousands of them in the care of the army throughout the Confederacy. The question as to what should and could be done with the slaves once they were free had engaged the attention of many Northerners, and various proposals were considered. Lincoln had advocated colonization. Schemes to send the Negroes to Africa, Central and South America, Mexico, the West Indies, and Texas were discussed but abandoned. A proposal to apprentice large numbers of them for a period of five years to construct the Union Pacific Railway and suggestions that they be helped to migrate to the Northern states were also discarded. It finally became the settled policy of the government that the slave population was to be kept in the South. The various military commanders were therefore faced, for the duration of the war, with the problem of feeding and finding employment for a vast army of Negroes. Various expedients were tried. Work camps were established, and some slaves were put to work building fortifications, others in planting cotton; still others were inducted into the armies.

The most extensive and influential volunteer effort to aid the Negroes was undertaken very early in the war—in fact, just seven months after the firing on Fort Sumter, when the Union forces occupied Port Royal and the string of Sea Islands along the coast of South Carolina. This was a rich cotton-growing area made up of some two hundred plantations. The slaveowners and the entire white population fled, hurriedly taking a few possessions and some household servants after setting fire to piles of cotton bales. The ten thousand or more slaves left behind were completely disorganized, and shortly were in need of food and clothing and some system of organization and management. The Port Royal experiment which followed was in many ways to be a testing ground for the future work of the Freedmen's Bureau.

Two major volunteer groups in New York and Boston took over responsibility for the work on the Sea Islands, which was centered in the small town of Beaufort. In New York, the American Missionary Society interested prominent abolitionists, and the National Freedmen's Relief Association was organized to undertake the task of recruiting volunteers and financing some of the costs of the project. This group's great objective was "to teach the Negroes Civilization and Christianity as well as order, industry, economy and self reliance; and to elevate them on the scale of humanity by inspiring them with self respect." [3] This was a rather large order, and the volunteers selected to go to Beaufort scarcely realized the difficulties they would encounter in carrying out so grandiose an aim.

In Boston, leaders in the community formed the Education Commission to carry on the Sea Islands program. Later a successor organization, the New England

[3] Quoted in Willie Lee Rose, *Rehearsal for Reconstruction: The Port Royal Experiment* (Indianapolis: Bobbs-Merrill Co., 1964), 41.

Freedmen's Society, was an active participant. The young men selected from Boston were graduates of the New England colleges and seminaries and were mostly Unitarian in religious affiliation. Friction between the evangelical zeal of the New Yorkers and the Unitarian outlook, with its emphasis on the virtues of hard work and good deeds rather than theology, created dissension on the islands. Such denominational differences were only the forerunners of the difficulties with which the Freedmen's Bureau had to cope in dealing with a variety of missionary groups after the war. However, the strong belief in emancipation held by all the Port Royal volunteers somehow kept them together in a working relationship throughout the war.

A total of fifty-three volunteers—twelve of them women—constituted the first group to arrive in Beaufort. Some became disenchanted and returned to their homes, but others, including a group from Philadelphia, volunteered. Altogether several hundred persons, mostly young men, participated in the Port Royal experiment. In many respects they constituted an early domestic Peace Corps. The distribution of food and clothing was an immediate task. The stately homes of many of the plantation owners in Beaufort had been pillaged and partly destroyed by the slaves; these were made more habitable for use as schools and as living quarters for the volunteers. The abandoned plantations were confiscated, and it was here that the first attempt to cultivate cotton on a large scale under a free labor system was undertaken. The establishment of schools where illiterate Negroes, young and old, learned to read and write was perhaps the most successful of the efforts to bridge the gap between slavery and emancipation.

It is difficult to evaluate the Port Royal project in terms of success or failure. Many of the aims of the original volunteers were unrealistic and subject to human frailties from the standpoint of the participants as well as of the slaves. Only the most dedicated volunteer could accept the disappointments and endure the hardships and the isolation from friends, family, and a customary way of life. The project attracted considerable public attention and some criticism but had an influence on federal policy for the reconstruction of the Southern states. Prominent social reformers associated with the freedmen's organizations urged Lincoln to establish a bureau of emancipation, arguing that in freeing the slaves the government had a responsibility for their care and protection. They realized that the need was immense and was beyond the resources of voluntary groups. Only the nation as a whole could undertake such a task. General Oliver O. Howard, who was to become the head of the Freedmen's Bureau, visited the Sea Islands several times, and the influence of Port Royal on the future program of that agency is evident.

The bill to establish the Freedmen's Bureau was a controversial one. Its constitutionality was a thorny question to many lawmakers, for this was a proposal to extend "charity" to the needy on a large scale and for the first time to tax the citizens of one state for the support of the destitute population of other states. Fear of the centralization of power in the federal government was another familiar issue raised by the opposition. Moreover, the motives of influential members of Congress were mixed. Divergent points of view as to how the former slaves and their masters were to be treated plagued the work of the bureau throughout its existence. The bureau was placed in the war department, and the act provided that it would cease to exist one year after the end of the war. A commissioner and ten assistant commissioners to direct the work in the states were to be appointed by the President with the consent of Congress and were made responsible for the administration of a complex and always controversial program extending over the lives of some three to four million former slaves, and eventually of many whites.

Oliver O. Howard, a West Point graduate and commanding general of the Army of Tennessee, was made commissioner. For his operating staff members at the local level, or agents as they were called, he was initially dependent on army personnel detailed to the bureau by military commanders without prior consultation with the district commissioners. There were able and conscientious officers in the bureau, but many assigned as agents had no qualifications for the task and frequently were disinterested or even unsympathetic with the work of the bureau, and some were not only inefficient but jeopardized the good name of the agency through their personal behavior. There was constant turnover in personnel and there were never enough agents to administer a difficult

program either efficiently or effectively. The refusal of
Congress in 1865 to appropriate funds for relief purposes
or for salaries meant that the bureau was dependent on the
commissary general for rations, on the quartermaster
general for clothing, and on the surgeon general for hospital and medical supplies. General expenses were to be
met from the sale or rent of confiscated and abandoned
property. Such were the conditions under which the bureau undertook to render aid to masses of former slaves
and eventually to many whites in an alien territory.

Transportation home had to be provided for the freedmen and many displaced persons. The distribution of food
was urgent all over the South. Hospitals needed to be
supplied with physicians, food, and medicine, and additional facilities were set up in buildings confiscated by the
government. There were many orphans and dependent
children to be cared for, and small institutions were hastily
improvised, some of which bore Howard's name. Conditions in Alabama and Georgia were reported particularly desperate. According to one Atlanta newspaper account, some 35,000 men, women, and children in the
nearby counties were dependent on government food, and
many more in north Georgia were near starvation. A
newspaper reporter, viewing the distribution of rations
in Atlanta, provided a vivid account of the motley throng
of people standing around the bureau distribution center:
refugees returning to their homes, Confederate soldiers
recently released from Northern prisons, the crippled and
the wounded, worn and destitute men who had fought

bravely, and the widows and children who had been left behind. In some amazement he commented, "I cannot help but remark that it must be a matter of gratitude as well as surprise for our people to see a Government which was lately fighting us with fire, and a sword and a shell, now generously feeding our poor and distressed." [4]

The bureau's efforts to feed the hungry were not viewed as sympathetically by many planters and townspeople, who claimed that the emancipated Negroes would not return to work as long as free rations were available. The transition from slavery to a free labor system was not easily accomplished, and there is no doubt that many Negroes were demoralized and disillusioned. Large numbers had become accustomed to being fed and cared for in the army camps and were reluctant to return to work on the cotton plantations, and the dream of owning "forty acres and a mule" had proved illusory. Bureau agents drew up and supervised labor contracts, proposed a minimum wage (which was not adopted), imposed assessments on planters and their laborers, and organized work camps and farm colonies in their efforts to adjust Negroes to a radically different way of life. At the same time vigilance was exercised to combat "reenslavement" of the freedman by his former master. As for the distribution of food and clothing, Howard on orders from the secretary of war very shortly began instructing his agents to re-

[4] Quoted in Walter Lynwood Fleming, *Documentary History of Reconstruction* (Cleveland: A. H. Clark Co., 1906–1907), I, 23–24.

trench and to break up the freedmen's camps so as to prevent "pauperization." He then ordered that all relief except to freedmen and refugees in the hospitals and orphan asylums was to be discontinued by October, 1866.

A series of disasters struck the South in 1866–67, and the situation became more desperate than it had been at the end of the war. Two tornadoes swept the South Carolina coast, destroying crops. Floods inundated large areas of the Louisiana plantations, also destroying crops estimated at $30,000,000. There were crop failures in other Southern states. Starvation among the population was reported imminent in many localities. Even Southern whites arose to protest the withdrawal of relief, for many of them as well as the Negroes were destitute. The agitation resulted in the passage of new legislation over President Andrew Johnson's veto in July, 1866, extending the life of the bureau for two years. This act provided the first direct appropriation for the work of the bureau, in the amount of $6,944,450, and made possible the use of civilian employees.

Early in 1867 a bureau assistant again predicted that hunger would soon be widespread in the South. In March famine was reported in the Carolinas. One of the bureau agents in New Orleans begged that relief not be discontinued. He said that although relief work was tiring labor, it was imperative to continue in order to prevent starvation of large numbers of persons during the approaching winter. He observed that the city treasury was so empty that the city could not even pay its employees and that the state was likewise unable to help. Whether or not such statements exaggerated the actual situation, there is no doubt the relief program of the bureau was still urgently needed. Howard tried to secure a new appropriation of a million and a half dollars with which to continue the distribution of rations during the next five months. Congress refused his proposal but authorized him to use bureau funds on hand to prevent extreme want for all classes of destitute or helpless persons in the South. Thus a far-reaching policy was established, enabling the bureau to aid Southerners of both races without regard to their Civil War loyalties. Gradually the need lessened and by January, 1869, the issuance of rations was limited to a few hospitals and orphan asylums. Other aspects of the bureau's work continued on a decreasing scale until June, 1872, when the agency ceased to exist.

As for the administration of the relief program at the grass roots, it must be emphasized that too few people were available to carry out the multitudinous tasks imposed upon the bureau. In general, the staffs were expected to protect the Negroes in their civil rights, to serve as magistrates with extraordinary judicial powers, and at the same time to cultivate amicable relations between the two races. The locating of missing persons was of immediate importance. A major task was that of helping Negroes find work and supervising contracts made between them and their white employers. The agents were directed to treat as vagrants any who refused to accept employment. They were to take charge of abandoned lands,

to assist in organizing and maintaining schools, and lastly
to serve as overseers of the poor in their districts. One
agent complained that he had to travel two thousand
square miles to cover his territory without the help of a
clerk or soldier; yet in addition to his ordinary duties, he
was directed to take a census of blind, deaf, and handicapped freedmen in his district. Some agents engaged in
trying to persuade Negro couples who were living together to marry—with mixed success. Moreover, the
work of the bureau had to be carried out in the face of
suspicion on the part of many Southerners that the agency was in reality a creature of the army of occupation.
No wonder Commissioner Howard is reported to have
wryly commented that the agents were required "to settle in a few days the most intricate questions in reference
to labor, politics, economics etc. that have puzzled the
world for ages." [5]

An officer's manual issued to the assistant commissioners covered general procedures, and from time to time
Howard kept them informed of current bureau policies
through letters, circulars, and additional orders. However, since the staffs at the state level were allowed considerable discretion, various methods of relief administration were followed in different states. In some of the
larger cities soup kitchens were set up, and in others work
relief projects were tried. In the rural districts persons
often had to travel considerable distances for handouts of

[5] Quoted in Bentley, *A History of the Freedmen's Bureau,*
136.

corn, pork, and clothing. In some states planters were furnished with food for their laborers on the theory that the freedmen would be fed, the planters would be able to make their crops, and at the end of the year the bureau would be reimbursed for its expenditures. In sections of Alabama and Georgia where there was extreme suffering, bureau rations were turned over to the civil authorities for distribution. This plan did not prove satisfactory, as it was found that in some counties local politicians used the rations to get votes and that the relief did not go to persons most in need.

A Union officer assigned as a bureau agent to Greenville, South Carolina, for fifteen months during 1866–67 recorded in his journal a detailed account of the problems he encountered in carrying out the program of the bureau. He refers to the great amount of paper work which the office entailed; reports, records, and correspondence took up a considerable amount of his time. Apprenticeship records, orders from his superior officers, labor contracts, and other documents had to be filed without the help of a clerk. At the end of every month bureau agents were required to make out reports of "outrages" committed by whites against freedmen and similar reports of those committed by Negroes against whites. Each report was to be written in triplicate. This officer complained that during his fifteen months of duty, he filled out and certified ninety such documents. In addition, he was required to report the number of destitute freedmen and orphans and to provide a census of the blind, deaf, and other handicapped Negroes in his district, which covered two thousand square miles.[6]

This officer was particularly impressed with the desire of many freedmen to travel about; he regarded the furnishing of so much transportation as a nuisance. Families dispersed under slavery wanted to get together and some longed to be back in their former localities. Many Negroes, disappointed in their hopes for "forty acres and a mule," migrated from South Carolina seeking land. The officer estimated that a thousand freedmen left the districts of Pickens and Greenville to settle in Florida, Arkansas, and Louisiana, hoping for higher wages. As for the poor whites who came to his office for aid, he indicated little sympathy for their plight and referred to them as a wretched caste or as "mean whites" who begged. As was true of many agents in districts throughout the South, the work of the bureau was not of his choosing, and he was naturally eager to leave Greenville when orders came releasing him from such a difficult post.[7]

A study of the bureau's activities in Mississippi provides a detailed account of the difficulties faced by the assistant commissioner and his agents in that state. Colonel Samuel Thomas, who was first appointed to head the bureau, was considered an able officer and a wise choice for the position. The military commanders had been forced during the war to make some provisions for feed-

[6] J. W. deForrest, *A Union Officer in Reconstruction* (New Haven: Yale University Press, 1948).
[7] *Ibid.*

ing and putting to work a multitude of Negroes in Mississippi as well as elsewhere. It was important to Thomas in taking over this responsibility to establish good relationships with the military. Working alongside the army were representatives of Northern missionary groups and charitable agencies. To further complicate his position, treasury agents were authorized to seize captured and abandoned property which might be sold for taxes.[8]

General William T. Sherman's march across the state early in 1864 had left widespread destruction. It was estimated that 400,000 freedmen, many of them homeless, came under the care of the bureau. An agent was assigned to each county, rations were distributed, and many freedmen settled on home farms, as they were called. The bureau assumed responsibility for the medical care of the freedmen under exceedingly difficult circumstances. There were only three hospitals in the state where Negroes could be treated and one for refugees, with a total of seven doctors in attendance. Some treatment in the homes was provided where there was no hospital available, but freedmen in parts of the state were without any medical care. The salary of one hundred dollars a month for physicians, the rate allowed by the government, made it difficult to recruit and keep staff members, and the turnover was constant. The national policy of the bureau on medical care was in fact very stringent; only extreme cases could be treated. The freedmen were

[8] Clifton L. Janus, "The Freedmen's Bureau in Mississippi" (Ph.D. dissertation, Tulane University, 1953).

told not to depend too much on the government, to depend on themselves and aid one another. Many orphans and abandoned children were kept in the camps. Older ones were apprenticed and the younger children placed in three institutions. Those at Vicksburg and Natchez were under the control of the American Freedmen's Commission; the third, at Lauderdale, was supported by the Society of Friends.

Colonel Thomas repeatedly appealed for funds to pay better salaries to physicians, to provide better food for patients, and to increase the staff of the bureau, but to no avail. Very early in his assignment he reported to General Howard that many of the staff members he was forced by the military to employ were not qualified and had little interest in their work. Those who were able were often recalled to their posts by the military commanders before becoming familiar with bureau policies. In addition, charges of immorality, corruption, and neglect of duty were made against some agents. Inadequate office space and equipment and the number of reports and paper work required were further sources of irritation.

Moreover, the bureau officials had to carry on in the midst of a hostile community. They were berated by the press, and uncomplimentary poems, epithets, and articles calculated to arouse the white population were printed in the local newspapers. Although it was reported that less than one-third of the freedmen received rations, and although under orders from Washington great pressure was put on them to find employment, the bureau was accused of fostering idleness. Thousands of Negroes were said to have lost a year and a half of work during the period of the "handouts." There were a few instances of attacks on bureau officers, and one was shot and killed as he took an evening walk on the streets of Granada. Responsible citizens of the town condemned the act and steps were taken by the grand jury to apprehend the murderer, but several months later he was still at large. Thomas summed up the situation when he said that the bureau received little support from the government and was opposed by the governor and the legislature. The white population believed it to be antagonistic to their own best interests and were determined to rid the state of the agency and all its works.

It was not only in Mississippi that there was dissatisfaction with the relief program of the bureau. Complaints about the "idle" and "undeserving" and the "pauperization" of whole segments of the population, Negro and white, were general throughout the South. At one point Howard declared that he was going to require the counties to provide for their own paupers, but rather than see the freedmen starve he would continue to feed them. The counties were either unable or unwilling to take on such a large financial burden, and Howard's warning was ignored. It can be said that the relief program of the bureau had little if any permanent influence on the poor law systems of the Southern states.

Further mention should be made of the Northern voluntary associations which were active in the South during and after the war and of their relationship to the work of the bureau. These were the various freedmen's aid societies and Northern church groups who organized schools for freedmen, distributed relief supplies, and supported a few orphanages. These organizations had proved to be successful money-raisers. Since the bureau was in the beginning without funds to pay for teachers' salaries or for other services, it was in Howard's interest that they carry on their activities as supplementary to his program. The assistant commissioners were directed to cooperate with them and to urge that their work of relieving the poor and educating the children be continued.

Cooperation between bureau personnel and the organizations, however, did not prove to be easy. The various associations were competitive and jealous of their prerogatives. The freedmen's aid societies of Boston, New York, Philadelphia, and Baltimore had united to form the National Relief Association, but there were also the Western Freedmen's Aid Commission with headquarters in Cincinnati, the Northwestern Freedmen's Aid Commission in Chicago, and others, as well as many church groups. Again in 1865, to prevent duplication and overlapping, some of the associations combined, forming the American Aid Commission; others refused to join, and most of the religious organizations continued to operate separately. Howard's efforts to persuade all voluntary groups operating in the South to unite in the interests of efficiency and economy provides an interesting footnote to more recent efforts to accomplish the same end in the health and welfare fields. Whether or not his suggestion was feasible, in view of the background and financial support of these separate organizations it should be no surprise that it failed.

This brief description of the Freedmen's Bureau and the relief program cannot adequately convey the immensity of the need which faced the commissioner or of the tasks which Congress assigned to him. The far-flung relief efforts of the bureau to meet a critical situation in the face of great obstacles probably deserve more credit than blame. There was no past experience in the administration of mass relief on such a scale and under such difficult circumstances. Thousands of the destitute were fed and clothed, many received urgent medical attention, and some, if not all, orphaned and abandoned children were given a modicum of protection and care. Directors of the Federal Emergency Relief Administration in Southern states during the Depression might well sympathize with General Howard and his assistant commissioners and conclude after reading one of the histories of the bureau that their own task in granting aid to the unemployed and in organizing work relief projects was by contrast relatively simple. Present-day public welfare officials might also take note that their complaints about the burden of paper work in the administration of public assistance programs are not new and have proved to be a feature of large bureaucracies.

VI

New Orleans: A Metropolitan Record

THE PREVIOUS illustrations of local relief practices have emphasized the region's rural and small-town character, which was to predominate for many years. In the centers of population, more institutions and resources were naturally available, especially for the care of the aged, the infirm, and dependent children. New Orleans, until recent years the largest city in the South, is not a typical Southern city nor were its relief-giving methods necessarily similar to those of other urban areas. The record, however, so clearly demonstrates the social philosophy that private charitable efforts are superior to governmental aid that it is of interest to the social historian. The issue of private charity versus public responsibility and the use of tax funds for the support of the destitute has been a controversial subject in the United States. The issue was debated during the first half of the twentieth century in the mothers' pension movement and during the Depression period of the 1930's with the inauguration of the Federal Emergency Relief Administration.

New Orleans, perhaps more than other metropolitan areas, has been reluctant to accept public responsibility for the support of local welfare services, and this point of

86

view has continued up to the present. It has been pointed
out that Louisiana, in contrast to nearby Southern states,
had no compulsory legislation for the care of the destitute until relatively late (1880). This attitude toward
public responsibility may have originated in part in the
Spanish and French background of the early inhabitants.
The population of New Orleans and the southwestern
parishes was predominantly Catholic, and the traditional
reliance on private charity, which was more marked in
Catholic than Protestant countries, may have influenced
the prominent elements in the community.

In any event this attitude found public expression in
New Orleans during the severe yellow-fever epidemic of
1822, when the need for relief of the sick and destitute
was so extensive that the city council was forced to take
action. The "Board of Benevolence"—a group of private
citizens appointed by the mayor—was directed to open a
public subscription to aid the sick. The following appeal
by the mayor is typical of the attitude so long held by the
city fathers of New Orleans: "The number of poor persons who yet remain a prey to contagion, renders entirely
unequal the resources placed at the disposition of the municipal authorities . . . but in circumstances so grave and
injurious, public benevolence is much less effective and
less powerful than private charity, which like the sentiment that forms its source is an inexhaustible fund." [1]

The attitude of the elected officials merely reflected

[1] Quoted in Wisner, *Public Welfare Administration in Louisiana*, 27–28.

the general views of the public over the decades. The charitable impulse was not entirely lacking, and many citizens engaged in efforts to aid the poor and sick. The press and the clergy constantly extolled the virtues of private charity. Sermons and poems on the subject were printed in the newspapers, and money-raising advertisements contained maxims urging readers to give generously to a variety of causes. As we know, mutual aid was one of the earlier defenses against sickness and death, and there was a great number of such aid societies in the city. The French dominated, but there were associations to aid the German, Italian, Spanish, Swiss, Scottish, and Portuguese residents. Fraternal organizations, as well as Catholic, Hebrew, Protestant, and nondenominational groups, were also active, with limited institutional programs chiefly for the aged and dependent children.

Commendable as such volunteer activities were, they provided no substitute for a system of public relief. Funds were scarce, efforts were sporadic and uncoordinated, and altogether the charities of the day were totally unequal to the task of aiding large numbers of the city poor. In 1852, just a year before the most virulent of all the yellow-fever epidemics swept the city, public attention was called to the extent of human misery, especially among the foreign-born population, and the statement was made that nine-tenths of the burden of destitution over the state was to be found in New Orleans.

It is true that New Orleans, as a major port located in a semitropical climate near the mouth of the Mississippi

River, faced special health problems. Shipping and epidemic disease are closely associated, and "malignant, pestilential and infectious diseases" periodically ravaged the population. Charleston, Savannah, Natchez, Mobile, and other Southern cities had their share of epidemics—but none to the extent or duration of New Orleans. It is recorded that from 1793 to 1901 the city lost a total of 41,348 inhabitants from yellow fever alone. Cholera was frequently epidemic, and ship fever and smallpox took their toll in lives. During the terrible epidemic of 1853, 8,000 persons were said to have died, and the city was spoken of as a graveyard. In order to dispose of the bodies, long trenches were dug and coffins were buried three and four feet deep. Many businesses closed and normal living was suspended while men, women, and even children nursed the sick and dying.

Had the city and state authorities imposed adequate quarantine measures, much of the tragedy could have been prevented. Efforts to establish a board of health with powers to set up a quarantine station and isolation hospital outside the city had proved abortive. In 1823, only a year after a severe yellow-fever epidemic, the local chamber of commerce passed a resolution stating that quarantine laws and regulations were useless and injurious to the commerce of the city. Again in 1853, the city officials failed to act promptly at the onset of the epidemic. The Howard Association, a voluntary organization of young men, then acted independently, assuming the duties of a board of health. They published a proclamation to an-

nounce that an epidemic was raging, furnished daily statistics of interments to support their action, and undertook to provide care for the sick and dying. There was
another yellow-fever epidemic in 1858, and the one in
1878 was considered particularly severe. The last to
plague the city was a much milder epidemic in 1905. In
retrospect, one can only say that the failure of the city
government and leading citizens to take the necessary
action to prevent much of the misery and destitution resulting from epidemics still remains a stain on the annals
of the city.

It is not to be assumed that there was no free medical
care in the city during these years, for the present Charity
Hospital, a state-supported hospital since 1814, provided
treatment not only for residents but for thousands of sick
strangers as well. Founded in 1735 as *l'hôpital des pauvres
de la charité* and named the St. John, it is one of the oldest
and still one of the largest tax-supported general hospitals
in the country.[2] One annual report of the board states
that of the 10,325 patients admitted in 1858, only 350
were residents of the state. Included in the statistics for
that year were patients from thirty states, the District of
Columbia, and twelve foreign countries, with Ireland

[2] Nathaniel W. Faxon in his short history of hospitals makes
no mention of Charity Hospital. He lists the following as the
first hospitals in the United States to claim consecutive operation to the present: Pennsylvania Hospital, 1751–56; Philadelphia Dispensary, 1768; New York Dispensary, 1791. Faxon, "A
History of Hospitals," reprinted from the *Bulletin of the American Hospital Association*, January, 1929, p. 32.

alone accounting for over 4,000 admissions. The journals and writings of travelers to the city often provide interesting sidelights on the Charity Hospital population. One colorful account speaks of the Hindu, the native of sunny Italy, the Russians from their frozen lands, and the fiery Spaniard who held a congress of nations within the hospital. The well-known English writer Harriet Martineau, after her visit to the city in 1830, wrote, "Great numbers of sick and destitute persons are perpetually thrown upon the mercy of the inhabitants and that mercy is unbounded. I have reason to believe the sick are not merely nursed and cured but provided with funds before departing." [3] At various times governors of the state appealed, with little or no success, to states bordering on the Ohio and Mississippi rivers to carry some of the financial burden of treating their residents. Only Pennsylvania made a small contribution. Urgent requests to the federal government to establish marine hospitals in the outlying territory came to naught. The ancient disease of leprosy was still another health hazard, and the existence of an early lazaretto is mentioned in the records. Later, the present National Leprosarium, the only one in this country, was started by the state of Louisiana in Carville. In 1922 the United States Public Health Service assumed responsibility for its support.

Illness has always been a major cause of poverty, and the great burden of providing medical care and some re-

[3] Harriet Martineau, *Retrospect of Western Travel* (London: Saunders and Otley, 1838), II, 124.

lief for the sick poor left a mark on the welfare institutions
of New Orleans. In 1822 the city resorted to a subsidy system, which was to have an impact on the local social welfare pattern for over a century. The first subsidy
(or "city alimony," as it was called) was paid to the Poydras Female Asylum when the twenty-four orphans in
the Ursuline Convent transferred to that institution. Every epidemic, both yellow fever and cholera, left many
orphans to be cared for, and new orphanages were founded soon after the epidemics of 1817, 1822, 1832, 1839,
1843, and 1853. These institutions and the homes for the
aged established later received small lump-sum payments
from the city and thus the pattern of institutional care
became intrenched. The fact that the state government
also made small lump-sum payments to New Orleans institutions further consolidated the subsidy system. Beginning in 1816 with an appropriation of $2,000 to the Poy-
dras Asylum, the number of grants greatly increased by
1855, although the individual sums were never large. In
1870 the legislature refused to make such appropriations,
and in 1879 the state aid to private charities became un-
constitutional. The discontinuance of state appropriations
to New Orleans institutions may have influenced the attitude of the city council toward their subsidy system, for
when a new city charter was under discussion in 1870 one
legislator declared that "he did not consider that the
Council were bound to support all the orphans and
poverty-stricken people of the city." He argued that "to
deprive private citizens of an opportunity of exercising

their benevolence was to do them an injury. . . . The poor were a legacy left us by the Savior himself. When we came here as administrators of a public trust like the directors of a bank or the managers of an insurance company, we had no right to give away in charity the money with which we were intrusted. . . . Why were we giving fourteen dollars a year for every orphan in an asylum . . . ?" [4] However, the city council renewed the appropriations. After 1900 the trend in the number of subsidies increased, with new agencies added to the list. The fact that every important institution in the city was already receiving a subsidy made it difficult to refuse new boards (which were often formed to duplicate services already established).

There was in the meantime no almshouse for the care of the aged and infirm until 1860, and then only as the result of a charitable bequest. The city government had made no effort to provide a public facility for the care of the most helpless of the destitute. During the first year of the Civil war a free market to supply food to those families whose fathers and sons had taken up arms was promoted with the slogan "the poor you have always with you"; it was reported to have aided eighteen hundred families. Local citizens and even slaves on the nearby plantations contributed produce "to feed the families of our gallant soldiers, who were battling against the

[4] Quoted in Evelyn Campbell Beven, *City Subsidies to Private Charitable Agencies in New Orleans* (New Orleans: Tulane University, 1934), 25.

fanatics of the North, the oppressors of the South and
enemies of the slaves." [5] When General Benjamin F. Butler occupied the city in 1862, the almshouse was taken
over for military purposes. It was completely destroyed
by fire toward the end of the war, and was not replaced
until 1878 when through the efforts of Mayor Joseph A.
Shakespeare a portion of the income from gambling li-
censes made possible the erection of a new institution.
However, it was not until 1915 that the city was able to
settle its old claim of $96,000 against the federal govern-
ment for destruction of the almshouse for the sum of
$21,000.

Butler found the city in a deplorable condition; according to his biographer, many of the inhabitants were near
starvation. Wives and children had no support with their
men away in the Confederate armies. City taxes were a
million dollars in arrears and the city government was
said to be spending its energies in frustrating Butler and
his officers, rather than aiding the poor. Among his several
general orders on the condition of the poorer inhabitants
of the city is the following criticism:

The deplorable state of destitution and hunger has been
brought to the knowledge of the Commanding General.
He has yielded to every suggestion made by the city government and ordered every method of furnishing food to the
people of New Orleans that the government desired. No re-

---

[5] Report of the Committee of Free Markets of New Orleans,
quoted in Beven, *City Subsidies to Private Charitable Agencies
in New Orleans,* 16–18.

lief by those officials has yet been afforded. This hunger does not pinch the wealthy and influential, the leaders of the rebellion, who have gotten up this war and are now endeavoring to prosecute it, without regard to the starving poor, the workingman, his wife and child. Unmindful of their fellow citizens at home, they have caused or suffered provisions to be carried out of the city for Confederate service since the occupation by the United States forces.[6]

General Butler went on to use even harsher words to indict the well-to-do classes of the city. A yellow-fever epidemic appeared imminent and he conceived the idea, a very good one, of employing the poor to clean the unsanitary streets and squares of the city, thus inaugurating an early work relief project. A series of orders was issued: the city was to employ two thousand men with families to work on the streets under competent supervision, each man to be paid fifty cents a day from city revenues, with a larger wage for skilled labor. In addition, the United States government would issue a full ration containing fifty ounces of food for each day's work. No one who had served in the Confederate forces was to be employed unless he took an oath of allegiance to the federal government. These measures proved inadequate to meet the extensive needs of the unemployed and on August 4, 1862, Butler issued his famous general order (or infamous, as it was regarded locally) imposing an assessment on certain persons, business firms, and corporations

[6] Quoted in James Parton, *History of the Administration of the Department of the Gulf* (Boston: Ticknor and Fields, 1866), 305.

of the city, probably the first attempt to tax local citizens for the relief of the unemployed poor of this city. It was recorded that nearly $300,500 was raised from this source. However, all of Butler's measures to feed the hungry did not meet the vast need throughout the occupied city. It was said that planters and other persons in the surrounding territory were without food and that hundreds, perhaps thousands, flocked to the city where rations were distributed by the army. In December, 1862, Butler reissued his order assessing local firms on behalf of the continuing relief needs, but there is no record in his biography of the amount raised. The state supreme court later ruled that General Butler's orders compelling holders of defense bonds to pay a certain percentage for the poor of the city was in fact punitory and that there was no action to recover such an assessment.[7]

With the end of the war the Freedmen's Bureau took over the task of feeding the former slaves and some whites as well. The year 1867 was a particularly bitter one for the inhabitants of New Orleans and the state. Floods from the Mississippi River caused great damage and some loss of lives. It was said, perhaps with some exaggeration if one considers the great yellow-fever epidemic of 1853, that "There never was a time in the history of Louisiana when so many people were near starvation."[8] Gen-

[7] *Anatole Cousins* v. *Abat Generes and Co.*, 21 La. 705 (1869).
[8] Quoted in Howard Ashley White, "The Freedmen's Bureau in New Orleans" (M.A. thesis, Tulane University, 1950), 44.

eral failure of crops on the nearby plantations increased the suffering; even the assistant commissioner of the Freedmen's Bureau (whose sympathies had naturally been with the Northern cause) recognized that the plantation owners were unable to pay wages or feed or clothe the former slaves employed to pick cotton and other crops. As though the situation were not desperate enough, there was another yellow-fever epidemic. More than 2,500 inhabitants of the city were said to have died from the fever, including several bureau agents. Again the Howard Association was active in attempts to aid the sick and destitute.

Before its program ended in 1868, the Freedmen's Bureau had distributed relief in kind; had aided some of the asylums for dependent children, along with the Northern Freedmen's Association; had established a temporary freedmen's hospital; had set up a dependents' home; and had taken over two hotels for refugees (apparently transients, as we would designate them today)—always a relief problem in this city. Before the bureau agents left, they urged the city government to take up the task of aiding the destitute. But in view of the depleted city treasury, there is little evidence that the officials were willing or able to assume such a burden.

New Orleans did not for many decades regain its prosperity of the pre–Civil War days, and there are recurring accounts of the extensive poverty in that city. A few textile factories were established in the latter half of the nineteenth century, largely dependent on the cheap labor of women and children. But the growth of industry was too slight to absorb the great numbers of unemployed. The prolonged depression of 1873 swelled the ranks of the unemployed and brought great suffering to many inhabitants. The city council was petitioned to employ those without work on public projects and a few were relieved in this way, but the problem of aid for the majority was unsolved. Nearly 2,000 men, women, and children were reported to have been sent into the country to work at low wages on the plantations, and 3,500 of the old and decrepit were furnished meager rations of flour, meal, and rice. Again, in the financial panic of 1893, the story of unemployment and misery was repeated. One newspaper reported that many Negroes and whites tried to keep body and soul together on thirteen cents a day. During this depression, New Orleans rebuilt the workhouse and restored the chain gang to deal with its many transients, who were often arrested by the police.

In 1883, a few local citizens with some recognition of the relief needs in the city had formed what was to become a new type of charitable agency. It was named the New Orleans Conference of Charities. An office was maintained to receive applications for relief, and district committees and a volunteer corps of women undertook friendly visiting among the poor. The object of this new organization was "to protect the community from imposters and mendicants, to reduce vagrancy and pauperism and to ascertain their true causes, to prevent indiscriminate and duplicate giving, to see that all deserving cases of destitution were properly relieved, to elevate the home-life, health and habits of the poor, and to prevent children from growing up as paupers." [9] The following year the Ladies Unsectarian Aid Society was formed as an arm of the conference to give out food, clothing, and coal, leaving the former organization free to make investigations of applicants, to keep records, and to handle correspondence. There were about seventy members of the society, and any "lady" who gave at least ten cents a week or regularly contributed groceries or assisted at the office for two hours a week was considered a member. Other money was raised through fairs, special appeals at Christmas, and other typical fund-raising methods of the period. It is no wonder that this voluntary charity could make no dent on the extensive poverty throughout many sections of the city, for its first report shows that only $298.65 was spent that year.

In 1897, a special session of the National Conference of Charities and Corrections in the city stimulated the reorganization of these various societies into a single body, the Charity Organization Society, which presumably was more nearly to meet the needs of the destitute and to do so along more constructive lines. Although under enlightened leadership, for the period, and with a better understanding of the plight of the unemployed, this agency never had anywhere near sufficient financial resources

[9] Quoted in Gladys Soulé, "The History of the Family Service Society of New Orleans" (M.S. thesis, Tulane University School of Social Work, 1947), I, 18.

to accomplish its relief aims. Then and now voluntary efforts were insufficient to meet a problem requiring the expenditures of tax dollars if the needs of the poor were to be met. The year 1897 brought still another yellow-fever epidemic, and perhaps for that reason the city council passed an ordinance providing that certain license fees be used to constitute a mayor's charity fund. The expectation that such a fund doled out by a clerk would answer the relief needs in a city of 300,000 inhabitants was obviously unrealistic. A study showing expenditures for public aid in six cities of comparable size reported that in New Orleans the amount was "trifling," that is, .01 per capita of the population or three cents per person.[10]

· An important factor in the attitude of the city officials has been the division of responsibility between state and local levels of government in the financing of health and welfare services in Louisiana. Since 1814 the state has assumed the cost of supporting the large Charity Hospital, which serves as the only municipal hospital in New Orleans, as well as admitting patients from other parishes. Free medical care for those unable to pay has usually been the responsibility of local governments, but New Orleans has been almost entirely free from this responsibility. Likewise, in the present public assistance program, which is state-administered, the four categories of public assistance are financed from state and federal funds, and

[10] Almy Frederick, "The Relation Between Private and Public Out-door Relief," *Charities Review*, VIII (March, 1899), 27. This study was made in 1897.

the state bears the cost of general assistance (which is limited to unemployables). Therefore, the parish officials have developed little tradition in meeting the heavy costs of local medical care and public aid. When pressed to appropriate funds for relief purposes, the New Orleans authorities tend to say "let the state do it." The city in 1970 appropriated $29,248 for temporary assistance, which is administered by the city department of public welfare. Here, in brief, is the main outline of the ways one Southern city dealt with poverty in its midst. It has been included in this study to indicate the long shadow historical events cast on social welfare patterns and that "what's past is prologue" to the present.

VII
Postwar Reforms

THE EXPERIENCE of defeat, military occupation, and
the political turmoils of Reconstruction resulted in a prev-
alent inertia and stagnation in many Southern communities. Reconstruction came to an end in 1877 and with it
gradually a modest recovery in the economy and a more
energetic and optimistic outlook on the part of the people.
This is the beginning of a period which historians, with
some reservations, refer to as the "New South." During
the period from 1820 through the 1840's, limited social
reforms had been made, influenced by contemporary
movements in the North and abroad, such as the abolition
of imprisonment for debt and better care of the mentally
ill; but generally speaking, Southerners lacked the reform-
ing zeal so strong in New England. As the historian
Arthur M. Schlesinger has said, in noting that the rhythm
of reform has differed in various parts of the country,
"more than any section [however] the South has resisted
innovation. As slavery tightened its hold on the region
and dimmed the ideals of the Revolutionary era, the people came to fear reform in general through fear of reform
in particular—that one which would destroy the rock on

which their society rested." [1] He goes on to point up their defense of slavery as a Christian institution and their resistance to the so-called isms of the North.

The South had long been a fertile field for missionary efforts both during the Civil War and afterwards. In the first decade of the twentieth century, Northern philanthropists by the score came to lend their money and their efforts to the "redemption" of the South. Walter Hines Page, the noted journalist and statesman and a North Carolinian by birth, returned to that state to undertake a crusade for the reconstruction of the South. In an 1897 address entitled "The Forgotten Man," he declared that the politician and the preacher had failed to solve the baffling social problems which retarded the South. Prominent Northern philanthropists and an official of the Rockefeller philanthropies agreed with these sentiments. In the spring of 1901 a special train loaded with such men came South and for a decade similar journeys were to be an annual event. A story of this venture was published in a New York paper under the caption "Men of Millions to Redeem the South." Inspired by the spirit of *noblesse oblige*, Southerners who were not millionaires but middle-class professionals, clergymen, and members of women's clubs, joined the ranks of the social reformers. There was, in fact, "enough to keep trainloads of philanthropists and batallions of uplifters busy in the South. Antiquated

[1] Arthur M. Schlesinger, *The American as Reformer* (Cambridge: Harvard University Press, 1950), 20.

social institutions protruded like primeval rock from smooth pavement to obstruct the traffic of progress." [2]

Then, as now, education was seen as the solution to the ills of the South, and the extension of universal public education in an area where free schooling had too often been regarded as a charity was the first challenge. Public schools were miserably supported and poorly attended, and the illiteracy rates were scandalously high. The system—if it can be called that—was, of course, biracial, a feature which added to the cost.

Even in the face of valiant efforts by Southern educational leaders and their Northern supporters, it is doubtful that a satisfactory system of public education or social services could have been financed in the Southern states at this time. The per capita wealth in 1880 was estimated at $395, as compared with $1,086 in the states outside the region. In 1883 a bill to provide federal aid for education was introduced in the Senate by Henry W. Blair of New Hampshire. It provided for ten annual appropriations, beginning with $15 million and diminishing by $1 million each year, to be granted to the states based on their ratio of illiteracy. Therefore the South would have received the major share of the appropriation, and it was estimated that for the first year $11 million would have been available for the Southern schools. This was more than the total amount spent for public education in the region in 1880.

[2] C. Vann Woodard, *Origins of the New South, 1877–1913* (Baton Rouge: Louisiana State University Press, 1951), 397.

This helpful proposal, which might have aided public education substantially, was debated in Congress over the next five years and then finally shelved. Efforts to improve public education went on and gains were slowly made, but the high birth rate was a retarding factor. The South has been referred to as the "seed bed" of the nation, and in an area with a low per capita income it has been difficult to provide not only education for so many children but other public services as well.

With the movement of Northern capital and the cotton textile industry Southward, seeking cheap labor, the great crusade to control child labor began. The poor and dispossessed flocked to the new mill villages, which sprang up in sections of Alabama, Georgia, and the Carolinas. Some became self-contained communities with their own schools, churches, recreational facilities, and mill-owned houses. The paternalistic attitudes of the millowners toward their employees served to strengthen the loyalty of the labor force in an area of the country where trade unionism was weak. Full-time staffs were employed in some of the Carolina mills to carry on what is usually referred to as industrial social service. They were not trained in any special field. A YMCA or YWCA secretary, a schoolteacher, or some local citizen (usually a woman engaged in volunteer work) was selected to direct the activities on a paid basis. This program to deal with some of the social needs of the mill workers—and to keep them contented with their lot—obviously ran counter to reform efforts on behalf of the men, women, and children who labored long hours at pitifully low wages in the mills.

The movement to enact child labor laws in the South was led by the American Federation of Labor and by Southern liberals. Edgar Gardner Murphy, a young Episcopalian minister from Montgomery, was the foremost Southern champion of this cause. He organized the Alabama Child Labor Committee, the first of such state organizations in the country, and was one of the founders of the National Child Labor Committee in 1904. In a region where malaria, hookworm, and pellagra were endemic and where tuberculosis and syphilis rates were high, the lack of public health protection was another challenge to the reformers.

Prison reform, along with the attempts to control child labor, was the most vigorous of the social welfare movements during the late nineteenth and early twentieth centuries, when the struggle against the convict lease system engaged the interest of many Southerners. The period following the war was one of great increase in disorder and crime, not only in the South, where conditions were abnormal, but in the Northern states as well. Southern penitentiaries had been partially destroyed or had fallen into disrepair, and the state governments faced the cost of rebuilding the institutions, not only for white prisoners but also for Negroes, who formerly had been largely subject to the plantations' penal system. As an expedient, the leasing of prisoners under various contracts was introduced in one state after another (in Louisiana the first lease dated back to 1844) by the provisional and military governments. The practice continued under the carpetbag regimes and by the state governments after the end of Reconstruction.

It was a cruel and politically corrupt system. Leases extending over ten or twenty years and longer were made to corporations, Northern syndicates, and politically powerful individuals. The state governments were concerned with the profitable employment of the prison population and with saving money, the lessees with making a profit from the labor of the prisoners. That the system was profitable to some lessees is indicated by a newspaper advertisement seeking bids on a Tennessee lease. The terms called for an annual payment by the lessee of $100,000 clear of all expenses to the state, except for the salaries of the warden, his assistant, the surgeon, and the chaplain, which would be paid by the state government. This illustration is typical of the system throughout the region, whereby private contractors were able to make a profit from the labor of thousands of adult offenders. As has been indicated, many Southerners opposed the cruelties inherent in the convict lease system. In Louisiana, for example, the system was a major political issue from 1878 to 1901, when a constitutional prohibition against the renewal of the contract forced the state government to take back control of the penitentiary. The first postwar lease had been sanctioned by Winfield Hancock, a Union general and chief of the military department of Louisiana and Texas, over the objection of Louisiana's governor. The Board of Control had been established to supervise the care given to the prisoners but was soon in conflict with the lessees and was never able to correct the worst abuses.

One of the outstanding figures to denounce the convict lease and contract systems was the author George Washington Cable, who had been born in New Orleans of slaveholding parents and had been twice wounded serving with the Confederate forces. In the midst of a successful literary career, he had become aware of prison abuses while he was serving on the New Orleans Grand Jury. He became active in trying to correct these and worked with the New Orleans Board of Commissioners of Prisons and Asylums to improve conditions in the orphanages and in other local institutions. Through study of reports from state penitentiaries, he became aware of the convict lease system. Cable familiarized himself with the current theories on penology and prison management both in the United States and abroad. He traveled throughout the South gathering facts on illiteracy rates, school attendance, crime rates, court sentences, and other matters that had a bearing on general social problems. In 1883 he gave a detailed report on prison conditions in the eleven Southern states before the National Conference of Charities and Corrections and was able to cite figures on the number of murders, drownings, and escapes, as well as the high mortality rate in each state. It was his conclusion that the system was at its worst in Arkansas, Mississippi, and Louisiana.

Cable went on to try to arouse the conscience of the public over the cause of Negroes, whom, he saw, did not receive justice in the courts of law. He had the courage to deliver a commencement address on "The Freedmen's Case in Equity" at the University of Alabama in 1884. He repeated the address, with some adaptations, before the American Social Science Association that same year. Cable wrote about the Negroes' right to vote, to hold office, and to serve on juries; about segregation in public transportation, schools, libraries, and churches; and about federal aid to education and federal intervention to protect the civil rights of Negroes. In short, Cable not only became a leading advocate of prison reform and the foremost Southern social reformer of the nineteenth century, but, in the opinion of a recent biographer, he published the fullest, most consistently developed statement for extending civil rights to Negroes that had appeared in this country.[3] His writings and public addresses were bitterly attacked by the Southern press. Although reluctant to withdraw from the controversy, he and his family moved to Northampton, Massachusetts, in 1885. He continued to visit the South and to believe that in time Negroes would gain their civil rights.

As for the treatment of the mentally ill, neglect during

[3] Arlin Turner, *George W. Cable: A Biography* (Durham, N.C.: Duke University Press, 1956).

the war and the period of Reconstruction left the state institutions far behind accepted standards of the period in their standards of care and left many, in fact, in a deplorable condition. For example, the annual reports of the board of the Louisiana State Hospital at Jackson described the buildings as dilapidated, with rotting floors, without heat, the water pipes rusty and leaking, and the water closets unusable. Appropriations to the hospital were made in depreciated state papers, and the salaries of the officers and attendants went unpaid. By 1876 the credit of the institution was exhausted and the board faced a debt of $40,000. The years 1875–77 marked the lowest ebb ever reached in patient care. So grave was the financial situation that the board suggested that the gates of the institution be thrown open and the patients allowed to go forth in the countryside to beg for their bread. Gradually funds became available and conditions improved, but it was several years before a modicum of treatment was instituted.[4]

The great increase in the number of Negro patients admitted to state mental hospitals after the war attracted considerable attention on the part of the medical profession during the late 1890's and the first decades of the twentieth century. Articles on insanity among Negroes were published in the professional journals, and one on "Psychoses in the Colored Race" estimated that while the Negro population had increased 111 percent during

[4] Wisner, *Public Welfare Administration in Louisiana*, 99–121.

the half-century from 1860 to 1910, the number of insane Negroes had increased 1670 percent.[5] These statistics are indeed startling, but they are of dubious value because in 1860 mentally ill Southern Negroes were not included in the then-official count.

In an address before the National Conference of Charities and Corrections in 1908, Dr. William F. Drewry, superintendent of the Virginia State Hospital for the Insane in Petersburg, an institution exclusively for the care of Negro patients, attempted to set forth the reasons for the great increase in psychoses among this group. Although he granted that there was doubtless some mental illness among the slave population before the war, his main thesis was that emancipation was largely the cause of the current problem. Dr. Drewry painted an idyllic picture of the Negro on the plantation, contented, well fed, and comfortably clothed, living an open-air life with wholesome employment, and cared for by his master when ill—all measures preventive to mental breakdown. Emancipation, he thought, had left him unprepared to care for himself and a prey to his passions. He had acquired habits of indolence and promiscuity, and the use of whisky and of cocaine and other drugs had contributed to his general decline. As a physician, Dr. Drewry was aware that better understanding of mental disorders tended to account for some increase in the commitment of Negroes as well as whites, but a review of his paper leaves one with

[5] Mary O'Malley, M.D., "Psychoses in the Colored Race," *American Journal of Insanity*, LXXI (1914–15), 309–37.

the feeling that in seeking to understand the problem his mind was set as to the basic cause.[6]

Later Dr. E. M. Green, clinical director of the Georgia State Sanitarium at Milledgeville, published a paper on the same subject. His analysis of the causes of the proportionally higher admission of Negroes to whites in that hospital since 1900 was based on a comparative study of a sizable group of patients and differed considerably from the speculations of Dr. Drewry. For instance, more disturbed Negroes than whites had later been diagnosed as suffering from pellagra. This nutritional disease was widespread in the South, and for obvious reasons more Negroes than whites were afflicted. Moreover, he had found that three times as many whites as Negroes were admitted for psychoses due to alcoholism and many fewer were found to be drug addicts. Dr. Green was convinced that the superstitions held by many Negroes influenced their behavior and affected their mental health.[7]

For whatever the statistics and diagnostic classifications of the period were worth—and they might well be questioned today—they are an indication of the growing concern over the ratio of Negroes to whites in the state mental hospitals. As the populations and resources of the states increased, the systems of care were extended and

[6] William F. Drewry, M.D., "Care and Conditions of the Insane in Virginia," *Proceedings of the National Conference of Charities and Corrections*, 1908, pp. 307–15.

[7] E. M. Green, M.D., "Psychoses among Negroes: A Comparative Study," *Journal of Nervous and Mental Diseases*, XLI, No. 11, pp. 697–708.

new institutions were constructed. Arkansas and Florida joined the other states in providing hospital facilities. The segregation policy continued and cut across all institutional care. Virginia, North Carolina, and Alabama had provided separate institutions for Negro patients; in the other states, Negroes were kept in detached buildings on the same grounds of the hospitals for whites or in annexes or separate wards.

A question little discussed today by social workers and public welfare officials which was of paramount interest in the earlier days is the care and treatment of individuals committed to the state institutions for the mentally ill and the state penitentiaries, and of the children in schools for the blind, for the mentally retarded, and for other handicapped groups. No attempt has been made in this study to trace the rise of state institutions in the South for handicapped groups other than the mentally ill. These individuals, usually helpless and inarticulate in regard to their own treatment in state institutions, were in fact "wards of the state," in Dorothea Dix's phrase. Unpaid lay board members were usually appointed by the governor, too often for political reasons, to supervise the administration of these institutions. Large public expenditures were needed to feed and clothe the patients and to run the facilities, and there was frequent graft by board members, as well as political interference imposed on the paid superintendents and staff. For various reasons, state institutions were often isolated in the country, away from the larger cities, resulting in a lack of public knowledge of and interest in their administration. There were occasional scandals over the treatment of inmates, particularly in the mental hospitals, and exposures of misuse of public funds in the administration of the institutions, but these seldom led to any permanent reforms. Although there were exceptions in all states, one can only conclude that in the past, the administration of many of our state welfare institutions (for a number of reasons) was often wholly inadequate and was frequently a disgrace—both in the treatment afforded those for whom it was intended and also in the amount of tax dollars appropriated to maintain these facilities.

What was needed was an overall view—a central authority to look into the provisions for the destitute. Also needed were persons in state and local institutions to ensure that inmates were receiving proper care, that tax expenditures were not wasted, and that the legislatures and public were informed about the discharge of the state's responsibility towards its disadvantaged citizens. The famous Massachusetts Board of State Charities, the first of the central authorities, was established in 1863, in the midst of the Civil War. A lay board of five members and a paid full-time executive (at a salary of $2,000 a year), or agent, as he was called, were directed to investigate and supervise the whole system of public charities and corrections of the commonwealth and to recommend changes and additional provisions as needed.

North Carolina was the first Southern state to provide such a central authority. In 1869 the General Assembly created the Board of Public Charities to supervise all charitable and penal institutions of the state. This was only six years after the movement for such central authorities was started in Massachusetts, and North Carolina's action was preceded by the creation of similar boards in only two other states, Ohio and New York, in 1867. Illinois, Pennsylvania, and Rhode Island established central authorities in 1869. When Dorothea Dix visited North Carolina in 1848, she had inspected a number of the county almshouses and jails. Her report to the legislature gave a vivid account of the terrible condition of the inmates in these institutions, but her interest centered on the neglect of the mentally ill and on the need for a state hospital, and she achieved her goal. The poor law practices went on as they had for many years. The war had intervened and the state was left impoverished and disorganized.

Members of the first North Carolina Board of Public Charities acted with vigor, visiting some of the counties and securing information from others, and they were shocked by what they learned about poor law practices. The first annual report of the board condemned the "whole system or want of system that seems to have grown up by accident and without benevolent concern for the welfare of the pauper class . . . and one that was unworthy of a Christian state." [8] The members appar-

[8] Quoted in Roy M. Brown, *Public Poor Relief in North Carolina* (Chapel Hill: University of North Carolina Press, 1928), 73.

ently concerned themselves with care of the destitute rather than the state institutions. Unfortunately this promising beginning in North Carolina was interrupted when the board ceased to function through lack of appropriations and failure of the governor to fill vacancies. In 1889 the board was revived and in 1917 reorganized as the state Board of Charities and Public Welfare. During the 1890's local volunteer committees were appointed to visit the almshouses and report to the board, and here and there they were able to report some improvements. However, later reports do not indicate any substantial reforms in the whole poor law system of the state.

At the onset of World War I, only six of the eleven Southern states had welfare boards with limited supervising powers over state institutions and agencies, but these bodies had little or no influence on the administration of local relief or almshouse care.[9] Later these early boards of charities and corrections became in many states the boards of public welfare, indicating a broader and more modern outlook.

The poor law systems of several states were to remain unreformed, as was largely true in the rest of the nation. In 1891 the North Carolina legislature sought to remove some of the stigma attached to poorhouses by designating them as homes for the aged and infirm, but in all the Southern states there were too few changes in the methods of aiding the destitute to be of significance. A dreary

[9] Alabama, Georgia, Mississippi, South Carolina, and Texas were without such central boards.

picture of the poverty of welfare resources in a small
Virginia town and throughout the state toward the end
of the nineteenth century is recorded in the reminiscences
of the first commissioner of charities and corrections. It
may stand as fairly typical of much of the South. The
local jail was dilapidated, filthy, and full of vermin. There
was no local relief for those in need and very little relief
organization over the state. Only the United Charities of
Norfolk attempted any systematic aid to the poor, and
there were one or two other private relief agencies staffed
by volunteers. The almshouses were receptacles for the
forgotten people, where they were fed and clothed at the
lowest possible cost while the officials waited for them to
die and then buried them without religious services in
paupers' graves. A few small orphanages were maintained
in the state, but many dependent children were taken into
families without any supervision or were sent to the
almshouses or even to the jails. Others shifted for themselves.[10] This description of the lot of the poor and discarded in one Virginia town may have been fairly typical
of conditions in many Southern communities.

Local responsibility and local tax expenditures for relieving the poor were not enough to ensure a humane
standard of care. The system was inefficient and wasteful
in human resources. Individuals, families, and children

[10] Lydia Gordon Shivers, "The Social Welfare Movement
in the South: A Study in Regional Culture and Social Organization" (Ph.D. dissertation, University of North Carolina, 1935),
Chaps. 4–5.

relegated to the almshouses or forced to live on pittances at home received no assistance in bettering their lot. Undoubtedly, some local officials were sympathetic and did the best they could under the circumstances of the time in aiding the destitute. But many appear to have been prejudiced toward this group, as was generally true of the taxpayers as well. Other poor law authorities were politically motivated and occasionally dishonest in administering relief.

THE CHARITABLE IMPULSE

In addition to the foregoing account of some of the post–Civil War movements in the South, reference should be made to the changes in the private charitable agencies which were influenced by Northern efforts to aid the poor. During the nineteenth and early part of the twentieth century there was an emergence of what has been called the "new poverty" in the larger cities of the North. This was caused in large part by rapid industrialization and the great wave of immigration from Europe. Leaders emerged to write about the misery of the poor in the slums and to urge various social reforms. *How the Other Half Lives* by Jacob Riis, which appeared in 1910, was a powerful indictment of conditions under which men, women, and children lived in the New York slums. This was only one of a number of books and articles, written over a half-century, about the increasing poverty in the large cities of the United States. The recurring economic depressions after 1819 had aroused public concern over widespread unemployment among the laboring classes. In response to these conditions many charitable societies flourished in the metropolitan areas. For instance, the influential New York Association for Improving the Conditions of the Poor, begun in 1843, was only one of thirty to forty charitable agencies already assisting the poor in that city. Similar developments were taking place elsewhere, especially in Eastern port cities.

Later, Northern missionary groups, as they had during the Civil War, turned their attention to the poor and ignorant in the benighted South. Their work in establishing churches, schools, orphanages, and social centers in the isolated mountain ranges of the Southern Appalachians would constitute a chapter in itself. It is also an interesting footnote to the current programs in Appalachia as a depressed area.

As for Southerners, while the charitable impulse was not entirely lacking, the region did not produce any of the great social reformers of the period. Because of the rural and semirural nature of the economy, with relatively little industrialization, and because of the institution of slavery and its aftermath, Southern attitudes toward social problems generally differed from those in the Northern cities. Moreover, the South never experienced the impact of the great European immigration that gave added impetus to social reforms elsewhere. Benevolent institutions and small relief agencies were established here and there, and various Protestant denominations founded hospitals, orphanages, and homes for the aged. Many of the clergy were fundamentalist in doctrine and powerful as revivalists. They had given sanction to slavery, yet paradoxically preached a gospel of mercy. Their acceptance of the "will of God" and emphasis on personal salvation often turned their attention away from the social conditions which they attempted to alleviate.

Catholic charities were influential in a few centers, including Mobile and New Orleans. Among the outstanding benefactors of the 1890's was Thomy Lafon, a Catholic Negro who left a substantial bequest to New Orleans institutions, three of which still bear his name. Jewish philanthropy in the same city and elsewhere had a long and distinguished record dating back to the middle of the century. Most of the charities were marked by the paternalistic attitude of the period, and their supporters were generally disinterested in any basic changes in the social structure of Southern society.

The Charity Organization Society movement, a national movement that originated in Buffalo, where the first society was organized in 1877, was to have a considerable influence on lay leaders in the larger Southern cities, where old relief societies were reorganized or new Associated Charities established. In the beginning the theme of "scientific charity," with its emphasis on investigation and on the elimination of indiscriminate almsgiving, must have restricted the treatment of those in need of help. In contrast to the old haphazard methods and sentimental attitude of the benevolent societies, the community was to be protected from exploitation by beggars and vagrants, and investigation by the Charity Organization Society would divide the deserving from the undeserving. In short, the new dispensation offered a systematic answer to old and baffling problems.

Whether or not all these new societies abided by the early C.O.S. principle—that their true function was to prevent duplication rather than to serve as relief-giving agencies themselves—cannot be stated. Like most of their counterparts in the North, although far less adequate in financial resources, the Southern societies became the major voluntary relief agencies in many cities. It has been said that the initial impact of the C.O.S. movement may have strengthened the negative thinking of the lay leaders sponsoring the new charities, some of whom had acquired wealth and were prominent in community affairs. Through contacts with the C.O.S. field staff members who visited the larger cities, board members and staffs developed a more progressive attitude toward people and their problems. The Atlanta Associated Charities, for example, founded in 1905 on the new wave of charity, became a progressive force in the Southern welfare field. A young lawyer, Joseph Logan, its first permanent secretary, was a rare person whose influence was felt in every social welfare movement in the state and elsewhere in the South.

The settlement house movement, which also originated in the North, was slow to take hold in Southern cities. The reasons are many. Undoubtedly there was a lag in providing the kind of neighborhood facilities usually associated with the social settlement, as was the case in other social service programs. Also, the founding of the famous settlements in New York, Chicago, and Boston was influenced by the great tide of immigration from the 1870's on, and Southern cities were largely untouched by the mass movement of Europeans to this country. Kingsley House in New Orleans, started in 1899, is now regarded as the first of the Southern settlements, although there were some earlier moves to provide small programs in Hampton, Virginia, and in El Paso, Texas. Eleanor McMain, who was head resident of Kingsley House from 1901 to 1933, was greatly influenced by Jane Addams and gave leadership to progressive welfare movements. The Southern School of Social Science and Public Service, a pioneer undertaking which Miss McMain promoted as a part of the settlement program, was the first center for training social workers in the South and was a forerunner of the Tulane University School of Social Work. Other settlements with substantial programs followed in Richmond and Houston. The organization of the Houston Settlement Association in 1907 resulted in the most extensive development in any Southern city. Consideration of the needs of such isolated groups as Negroes and Mexicans came much later.

One more comment on the strength and influence of the voluntary agencies is needed. In general, those in the South were without the benefit of large charitable endowments, which were a substantial help to many of the important social agencies in Northern cities. It is axiomatic that great philanthropies are the outgrowth of great wealth. Whether or not a tradition of bequeathing large sums for charitable purposes was strong in the South, it is evident that as a result of the Civil War and the near-destruction of the Southern economy, there was, for many years, little wealth to distribute for such causes.

VIII
The Social Welfare Conference

THE BIRTH OF the social welfare conference was of great importance in bridging the gap between the social service efforts of Southerners and the vigorous leadership of the National Conference of Charities and Corrections, the Charity Organization Society, and the settlement and child welfare movements. During and following the war Southerners interested in social problems had been isolated and without the stimulation of wider contacts and new ideas. The National Conference of Charities and Corrections, which became the National Conference of Social Work in 1917 and is now the National Conference on Social Welfare, has had a continuing influence on the development of social work and social welfare policies in this country. It was founded in 1873.

Before the 1883 meeting of the conference in Louisville, Kentucky—the first to be held in a Southern city—only one, two, or three delegates from the former Confederate states are listed as attending these yearly functions. At the annual meeting five years earlier in Boston, F. B. Sanborn, one of the secretaries of the conference, commented that he had made special efforts to enlist the support of Southern governors and personal friends to see that interested persons were appointed to attend. He thought the reason so few came was that in the South delegates were appointed by the legislatures whereas in the North the governors had the privilege of naming them. Sanborn's disappointment over the lack of Southern representation at the Boston meeting was justified, as only one Southern delegate was present, a minister from Charleston, South Carolina, who identified himself as a member of the American Missionary Association, connected with a children's home. Undoubtedly, Boston seemed remote and the cost of travel prohibitive for many Southern workers during this period. At the 1883 Louisville meeting, for the first time there was an increased attendance; thirty-four delegates, from nine Southern states, were present. Only Arkansas and Texas were not represented. In 1894 the conference met again in a Southern city, Nashville, and three years later there was a special session in New Orleans.

It was the Atlanta conference in 1903 that was to make the sharpest impression on the Deep South. Great preparations were made by local groups to ensure the success of this meeting. A local committee of one hundred men and sixty women was formed, and at their request, the governor appointed committees in a hundred Georgia cities and towns and urged the governors of other Southern states and mayors of cities to send delegates to the Atlanta meeting. The entertainment furnished the delegates at "the elaborate homes for which Atlanta was becoming famous" was so extensive that the conference had to rearrange its agenda to allow time off for such occasions.[1]

The president of the conference, the New York philanthropist Robert de Forrest, tactfully chose as the subject of his address "The South and the North Each Best Fitted to Solve Its Own Problems." He remarked that before preparing his speech he had consulted a gentleman close to public sentiment in the South as to what subjects should be avoided and was told to speak freely on any issue if it was dealt with in a national spirit. His further comment that the Negro problem was essentially a Southern problem and must be solved by Southern people was undoubtedly well received by the delegates. According to *Charities*, a weekly review published by the New York Charity Organization, this meeting attracted the widest editorial and press coverage of any social welfare conference up to that time. The following statement from the Atlanta *Constitution* was not only flattering to the delegates but caught some of the spirit pervading this meeting: "It is a distinguished body of citizens from many quarters of the land actuated by the highest principles of philanthropy and patriotism. It has served to introduce to our people for the first time persons of the most famous repute in American reforms and to furnish from their own lips the wisdom of humanity

[1] Alice R. Hamilton, "The History of the Department of Public Welfare of Georgia, 1919–1937" (M.S. thesis, Tulane University School of Social Work, 1939), 2.

. . . . That great good will accrue from the labors of this conference is assured." A reporter who covered the conference for *Charities* was impressed with the tolerant spirit in which the Southern press handled the rather sharp criticism of local social welfare institutions and practices by visiting delegates, who "went about with their eyes wide open and hesitated not to speak of what they saw." [2] Five years later, Richmond was selected for the annual meeting, and in 1914 the conference met in Memphis.

The opportunity to exchange ideas and to discuss new programs at a conference has always been a stimulating force in the development of social welfare services in this country. Southern workers had not only been isolated from their Northern colleagues but from each other, as the distances between the centers of population across state lines were considerable before the advent of the airplane. Actually, there were few paid executives or staffs, in the modern sense, to meet together, since the management of social agencies and institutions was largely in the hands of volunteer lay board members and church groups. With the emergence of state welfare conferences, local and statewide social problems came under discussion. It is of some interest that the first of these in the South and one of the earliest in the country was organized in Virginia in 1900 by twenty-four physicians and superintendents of the state mental institutions. Slowly other

[2] *Charities,* X (1903), 547–49.

state conferences emerged, with the social welfare group predominating.[3] Unfortunately, there is no available record of the early membership or the extent of influence they may have had on social welfare movements in the various states.

Of great importance at the time was the organization of the Southern Sociological Congress, which held its first meeting in Nashville in 1912 and which brought together some seven hundred delegates, mostly Southerners. The name of the congress is misleading, for the founders were not concerned with sociological theory but with poverty, prison reform, child labor, and similar problems throughout the Southern region. The originators were crusaders for social action to right the wrongs in Southern institutions. In fact, sociology as an academic discipline was undeveloped in the Southern universities of this period, and use of the term for the congress seems to have implied a more constructive approach to improving social conditions than the older benevolent system. At its loftiest it suggested "a methodical endeavor to regenerate and ameliorate society." [4] At the same time the moral and

[3] State conferences were founded as follows: South Carolina (1908), Texas (1909), Florida (1911), Arkansas and North Carolina (1912), Tennessee (1914), Alabama (1916), Georgia (1924), Mississippi (1928). *Social Work Yearbook, 1935* (New York: Russell Sage Foundation, 1935), 661–67. This source gives the founding of the Louisiana Conference as 1922, but the records of the conference indicate that it was organized in 1916.

[4] Quoted in Charles E. Chatfield, "Southern Sociological Congress: Rationale for Uplift," *Tennessee Historical Quarterly*, XX (1961), 51–52.

religious implications of many discussions are evident throughout the meetings of the congress. Northerners who attended the meetings were impressed by the religious fervor of many of the speakers.

The idea for this movement originated with Miss Kate Bernard, the personable and persuasive commissioner of the Oklahoma department of charities and corrections. On a visit to Nashville, she called on Governor Ben W. Hooper of Tennessee, urging him to issue a call for a Southern welfare conference. Governor Hooper had worked for better child labor legislation, for a parole system, and for removing the stripes from the uniforms of certain grades of prisoners, as well as for other progressive measures. For this reason his name was known to social reformers in other Southern states. The governor was persuaded and issued a call to the governors of sixteen states, requesting them to send one hundred delegates each to the Nashville meeting. His invitation stated that most of the annual meetings of the National Conference of Charities and Corrections had been held since its beginning in Northern cities, that the benefits had accrued to the Northern states, and that the discussions were from a Northern point of view. The slogan for this new organization was "The Solid South for a Better Nation," and it was thought that thousands of men and women, inspired by a patriotism for their beloved South, would volunteer in a crusade of social service. The organization started off auspiciously with a contribution of $7,500 from a local philanthropist, Mrs. E. W. Cole, to help meet the expenses of the congress. James E. McCulloch, a Virginian who had received his Bachelor of Divinity degree from Vanderbilt, was appointed secretary.

An executive committee was appointed, and the first question before the members was whether the congress should become a permanent organization. It was agreed that such a body would be invaluable in mobilizing Southern resources, encouraging native leadership, and arousing newspaper comment on social problems. There was also the practical consideration of the cost of traveling expenses for Southern workers attending annual meetings of the national conference. The decision was to make the congress a permanent body, with annual meetings to be held in conjunction with those of the national conference if and when such meetings were held in Southern cities. Unlike the national conference, which included memberships of many associations, the congress was an organization of individuals. Membership was based on payment of the required fee. It was heterogeneous and the interests of the members were largely unorganized and therefore not bound by organizational ties. This fact was a source of both strength and weakness in the congress as time went on.

The earlier programs of this congress were patterned after those of the National Conference of Charities and Corrections, with a number of prominent members of the conference as speakers. John M. Glenn, director of the Russell Sage Foundation; Graham Taylor, founder of the famous settlement, the Chicago Commons; and Edward T. Devine, director of the New York School of Philanthropy, were among those represented on the first program. These men had wide experience in the welfare field and therefore lent prestige to this first Southern conference. One has only to read the proceedings of this meeting to be caught up in the excitement of "this call of the New South," "this crusade for social service," "this battle for social betterment"—sentiments scattered throughout the conference speeches. There was some of the usual Southern oratory about the ordeal of the Civil War and its consequences, but on the whole a spirit of optimism pervaded the meeting. The South had advanced materially and the congress delegates no longer looked backward but now looked forward to a "New South." A critical spirit toward the solution of the region's social problems was perhaps the most important aspect of this first Southern social welfare conference. A defensiveness in the face of outside criticism, frequently latent in the Southerner, was significantly absent from the discussions. As the clergyman who gave the welcoming address said, "Tell us the truth about ourselves, remembering the while that we want curative remedies and effective surgery, as well as brave and accurate diagnosis." [5]

The meeting of the congress in Atlanta the following year was another solid achievement. The program was thought to compare favorably with that of the national conference, and eight hundred delegates were said to be

[5] James E. McCulloch (ed.), *The Call of the New South* (Nashville: Southern Sociological Congress, 1912), 20.

in attendance. The section on race problems included seventeen papers and was well attended by both whites and Negroes. The public proceedings ran to seven hundred pages. In 1914 the meeting was held in Memphis jointly with that of the National Conference of Charities and Corrections.

By prior agreement the usual conference subjects were the responsibility of the national body. The congress organized sessions on race relations and on the church and social service. The latter became a distinctive topic of the Southern Sociological Congress. A similar subject introduced by the national conference in 1911 had been discontinued, but the Southern version became increasingly important. Speakers in the race relations sessions were frankly critical of the economic deprivations of Negroes in the South and urged better educational and employment opportunities, equal justice, and improved health and housing conditions—all based on the underlying doctrine of "separate but equal." Desegregation was decidedly not the issue of the day. The congress had probably provided the first opportunity in the South for Negroes and whites to meet together in conference sessions and the first opportunity to welcome Negro speakers. At one point a Memphis session on race relations was adjourned from the Orpheum Theater, where the meetings had been scheduled, to a white church so that the Negro delegates could sit on the main floor with their fellow members. It is of some interest today to read that the National Association for the Advancement of Colored

People, meeting in a separate convention in Memphis, took the occasion to make a vigorous attack on both the congress and the National Conference of Charities and Corrections, presumably for their attitudes towards basic issues affecting the racial problem.

This was the last of the Southern Sociological Congress meetings to serve the interests of the social welfare members to any extent. The following conference in Houston carred the title "The New Chivalry—Health," and marked a turning point for the congress. The speeches regarding public health measures were delivered with evangelistic fervor, and the following chorus was sung (to the tune of "Tipperary"):

> It's a hard fight to save the children;
>> It's a hard fight we know.
> It's a hard fight to save the children,
>> But the fiend Disease must go.
> Come, men, for hearth and homeland,
>> Play up, do your share!
> It's a hard, hard fight to save the children,
>> But the Old South's right there.[6]

Following the meeting the officers decided to conduct a crusade to culminate in a great health congress the following year. The group was determined to eradicate malaria, hookworm, typhoid, tuberculosis, and other preventable diseases through an extensive campaign in South-

[6] Quoted in James E. McCulloch (ed.), *The New Chivalry—Health* (Nashville: Southern Sociological Congress, 1915), 12.

ern cities. The first regional meetings were held in Columbia, Tennessee, and subsequently in ten other Southern cities on a weekly basis. The purpose of the campaign was to stimulate local interest and action through revival-like exhortations to local committees and the public. A Pullman car was used to carry exhibits, literature, and speakers from city to city. What influence this crusade had on the development of the public health movement in the South cannot be stated, but at least those directly concerned were apparently pleased with their efforts. In 1916 the headquarters of the congress were moved from Nashville to Washington. World War I intervened and the membership declined. After 1919 the territory covered by the congress was divided, and the Southwestern Sociology Congress was organized as a coordinate body.[7]

The original platform of the Southern Sociological Congress, drawn up at the first meeting in Nashville, dealt with concrete social problems such as juvenile delinquency, prison reform, and child labor, and the programs were modeled on those of the National Conference of Charities and Corrections. As time went on there was apparently a shift in the leadership of the congress, with the clergy dominating the meetings. The programs became nationalistic in content with little focus, and were inspirational, rather than professional, in character. The program of the 1919 meeting in Knoxville illustrates this point. There

[7] The area represented included Arkansas, Colorado, Kansas, Louisiana, Missouri, Oklahoma, and Texas.

were a number of papers on public health and two on child welfare developments in Belgium and England, but none on the lack of adequate resources for dependent children in the Southern states. Other addresses bore such titles as "The Coming of Democracy," "The Practice of Citizenship," and "The Church Conserving Life." Again singing was an important aspect of this meeting, and three songs are printed in the proceedings. One entitled "Comrades," with ten verses sung to a Scottish tune, directed the audience to take a pledge by lifting the right hand while singing the last line of each verse, "Lift your pledge to God!" In 1920 the name of the congress was changed to the Southern Co-operative League for Education and Social Service. The group became increasingly concerned with what was called "home betterment," and in 1925 the name was again changed. The organization became the Home Betterment League, and this change marked the demise of the original Southern Sociological Congress.

It is difficult to evaluate the long-term contribution of the congress, which was launched with such enthusiasm only to decline through lack of effective leadership. As an indigenous Southern movement, it served in the beginning to bring together social service workers and social reformers who had been largely isolated from each other. The early meetings also brought some Northern social workers to the South, and although the results are intangible, these associations undoubtedly bore fruit in the long run. The original programs of the annual meetings included papers and discussions on current social problems. These were subjects of great interest to Southerners who attended the meetings, and the programs must have served as a stimulus to action at the local level. Especially significant for the period was the fact that the meetings were interracial. Moreover, the section on race relations with papers given by faculty members from several universities contributed to the thinking of the members.

It is not clear from the proceedings why the congress was, after only three years, taken over by the public health group. The prevention of communicable diseases was, of course, an important objective for a Southern movement but not the one set forth by the founders of the congress. The regional meetings organized by the public health members may have had an impact on the local communities where they were held; but what, if any, influence they had on the public health movement in the South cannot be stated. On the credit side, it should be pointed out that in addition to the Commission of Southern Universities on Race Relations, several local and regional groups were organized as a result of the congress meetings. These included the Tennessee branch of the National Conference of Charities and Corrections, the Conference on Law and Order (on lynching), the Southern District of the Travelers Aid Society, and the Southwide campaigns of the Anti-Saloon League. The published proceedings of congress meetings and the distribution of scores of public health leaflets probably had some influence.

There was perhaps a certain inevitability in the loss of interest on the part of the social welfare group, as participation in the programs of the American Red Cross during World War I brought Southerners closer into line with national movements and with the National Conference of Social Work (formerly the National Conference of Charities and Corrections). The Home Service Division of the Red Cross reached into every state and county and spread the message of individualized service and the casework methods of the period. For the first time in the South some training opportunities and paid employment on a wide scale were offered and new sources of personnel were tapped. This period marked the beginning of the professionalization of the social services in the region and helped promote professional education for social work. During the Depression such federal programs as emergency relief, public works, and social security made large funds available for the first time to states and localities for welfare programs. Federal leadership and standards brought the Southern states further into line with nationwide patterns. In short, it may be said that the South as a region was no longer set apart from the rest of the nation in its public welfare development.

BIBLIOGRAPHICAL ESSAY

CHAPTER I *The Colonial Period*

In contrast to the New England states, New York, and the Middle West, very little has been published about Southern measures for the relief of the destitute. Marcus W. Jernigan, *Laboring and Dependent Classes in Colonial America, 1607–1783* (Chicago: University of Chicago Press, 1931), Chap. 12 gives a brief account of the early poor law measures in Virginia. Roy M. Brown, *Public Poor Relief in North Carolina* (Chapel Hill: University of North Carolina Press, 1928) provides a detailed account of measures for the destitute in that state and has been referred to in several chapters of this volume. Elizabeth Wisner, *Public Welfare Administration in Louisiana* (Chicago: University of Chicago Press, 1930) provides an account of the relief measures in that state which are discussed in later chapters.

As for South Carolina, the statutes passed by the legislature served as the major reference to the poor laws. It was not the purpose of this chapter to trace them in detail since they varied little in content from those of other Southern colonies.

The section on the founding of the Georgia colony has largely drawn on the following: Daniel J. Boorstin, *The Americans* (New York: Random House, 1958), Part 3; Leslie E. Church, *Oglethorpe: A Study of Philanthropy in England and Georgia* (London: Epworth Press, 1932);

Myldred F. Hutchins, "The History of Poor Law Legislation in Georgia, 1733–1919" (M.S. thesis, Tulane University School of Social Work, 1940). See *The Autobiography of Benjamin Franklin* (Boston and New York: Houghton Mifflin Co., 1896), 132–33, and Grace Abbott, *The Child and the State* (Chicago: University of Chicago Press, 1938), II, 24–32 for information and documents relating to Bethesda. Henry Churchill Semple, J.S., *The Ursulines in New Orleans* (New York: P. J. Kennedy & Sons, 1925) tells the story of the beginnings of the Ursuline Convent as an educational institution, not an orphanage. It temporarily housed twenty-four orphans placed there until their transfer to the Poydras Female Asylum, the oldest child care institution in the city.

CHAPTER II
Relief in the Territories and States

For this section the author has relied heavily on unpublished masters' theses written under her supervision at the Tulane University School of Social Work: Ruby L. Hines, "Early Problems of Public Welfare Administration in Alabama" (1933); Dorothy Ann Hamm, "A Study of the Influence of Public Assistance Legislation on the Almshouse Population in Mississippi" (1947); Bernice Greaves Ratcliffe, "100 Years of Poor Relief Administration in Arkansas, 1836–1936" (1947); Helen Evans, "Provisions for Public Relief in Texas, 1841–1937" (1941).

Two masters' theses and a field study from the School of Social Service Administration, University of Chicago, proved helpful. They are Olive Mathews Stone, "Poor Relief in Alabama" (1929); Ellen Barbour Wallace, "History of Legal Provisions for the Poor and of Public Welfare Administration in Tennessee" (1927); Cleta Weatherby Davis, "History of

Public Welfare Administration in Florida" (1936). Nathaniel B. Bond, "The Treatment of the Dependent, Defective and Delinquent Classes in Mississippi" (Ph.D. dissertation, Tulane University, 1923) provided a limited view of the Mississippi legislation.

Harry M. Hirsch, *The Compilation of the Settlement Laws* (Chicago: American Public Welfare Administration, 1939) is a useful reference for this body of legislation as of the date it was published. Edith Abbott, *Public Assistance* (Chicago: University of Chicago Press, 1940) must be included as it is her analysis of the settlement and family responsibility regulations in the poor laws that provide the necessary background for any consideration of these questions.

CHAPTER III *Local Relief Practices*

In addition to the theses previously cited the following was especially useful in the discussion on the almshouse care: Anita Van de Voort, "Public Welfare Administration in Jefferson County, Alabama" (M.S. thesis, Tulane University School of Social Work, 1934). See also William Earle Cole, *Almshouse Policies and Almshouse Care of the Indigent in Tennessee* (Knoxville: Research Council, University of Tennessee, 1938).

As for measures for the relief of the civilian population during the Civil War, two masters' theses at Tulane University School of Social Work are useful references: Ruby Billingslea, "The History of Public Welfare Administration in Dougherty County, 1854–1930" (1947), and Pamela Elizabeth Robertson, "The History of Poor Relief in St. Landry Parish, Louisiana" (1942). For an interesting discussion of the Northern Civil War charities see Emerson David Fitz,

Social and Industrial Conditions in the North during the Civil War (New York: Macmillan Co., 1910), Chap. 11.

CHAPTER IV *Early Care of the Mentally Ill*

A general account of the early care of the mentally ill and the rise of the state institutional system is to be found in Henry Hurd (ed.), *The Institutional Care of the Insane in the United States and Canada* (3 vols.; Baltimore: Johns Hopkins Press, 1914). American Psychiatric Association, *One Hundred Years of American Psychiatry* (New York: Columbia University Press, 1944) was another useful reference. Also helpful was Albert Deutsch, *The Mentally Ill in America* (Garden City, N. Y.: Doubleday, Doran and Co., 1937).

The documents and reports relating to the many movements in which Dr. Benjamin Rush was engaged are to be found in the *Social Service Review*, II (1928), 469–86. Other documents about the establishment of the Williamsburg hospital in Virginia are included in Sophonisba P. Breckinridge, *Public Welfare Administration in the United States* (2nd ed.; Chicago: University of Chicago Press, 1938). Those documents about Miss Dix's efforts to secure federal funds for the mentally ill in the states are also included in this volume.

The biography *Dorothea Dix* by Helen E. Marshall (Chapel Hill: University of North Carolina Press, 1937), a useful reference, gives a limited account of Miss Dix's efforts in the Southern states.

Among her memorials to state legislatures, the best known is her first appeal to the Massachusetts legislature in 1848, which is included in Old South Leaflets, General Series, VI, No. 148. Other memorials, not discussed in Miss Marshall's biography, which resulted in the establishment of the Alabama and Mississippi state institutions are "Memorial Soliciting a State Hospital for the Insane, Submitted to the Legislature of Alabama, November 15, 1849," *Alabama House of Representatives Documents*, No. 2, and *Memorial Soliciting Adequate Appropriations for the Construction of a State Hospital for the Insane in the State of Mississippi* (Jackson: Mississippi Legislature, 1850).

CHAPTER V *The Freedmen's Bureau*

The general organization and program of the Freedmen's Bureau are discussed in the following references: Paul Skeels Peirce, *The Freedmen's Bureau* (Iowa City: University of Iowa Press, 1904); George R. Bentley, *A History of the Freedmen's Bureau* (Philadelphia: University of Pennsylvania Press, 1955); Walter Lynwood Fleming, *Documentary History of Reconstruction* (Cleveland: A. H. Clark Company, 1906–1907), Vol. I.

A number of studies provide useful information about the operation of the bureau in the Southern states and localities. They include Laura Josephine Webster, "The Operation of the Freedmen's Bureau in South Carolina," *Smith College Studies in History* (1916), Nos. 2, 3; Howard Ashley White, "The Freedmen's Bureau in New Orleans" (M.A. thesis, Tulane University, 1950), and his Ph.D. dissertation at Tulane, "The Freedmen's Bureau in Louisiana" (1955). Another Ph.D. dissertation, Clifton L. Janus, "The Freedmen's Bureau in Mississippi" (Tulane University, 1953) was particularly helpful.

For a detailed account of the administration of the bureau at the local level which was of special interest, see J. W. deForrest, *A Union Officer in Reconstruction* (New Haven: Yale University Press, 1948).

An interesting and authoritative account of the Port Royal experiment is to be found in Willie Lee Rose, *Rehearsal for Reconstruction: The Port Royal Experiment* (Indianapolis: Bobbs-Merrill Co., 1964).

CHAPTER VI

New Orleans: A Metropolitan Record

An account of the innumerable small private charitable efforts before the Civil War is included in Juliana Liles Boudreaux, "A History of Philanthropy in New Orleans, 1835–1863" (Ph.D. dissertation, Tulane University, 1961). My brief reference here to the volunteer work of the long-forgotten Howard Association does not do justice to this group of young men and their services in the 1853 yellow-fever epidemic. For a fuller account see Elizabeth Wisner, "The Howard Association of New Orleans," *Social Service Review*, XLI (1967), 411–18.

Evelyn Campbell Beven, *City Subsidies to Private Charitable Agencies in New Orleans* (New Orleans: Tulane University, 1934) covers the city subsidy system to private agencies in detail down to date of publication. For a description of General Butler's efforts to relieve destitution in the city during the Civil War see James Parton, *History of the Administration of the Department of the Gulf* (Boston: Ticknor and Fields, 1866), Chap. 18.

The continuing extent of poverty following the end of the Freedmen's Bureau program is discussed in Roger W. Shugg, *Origins of Class Struggle in Louisiana* (Baton Rouge: Louisiana State University Press, 1939). For a detailed history of the first modern casework agency in New Orleans see Gladys Soulé, "The History of the Family Service Society of New Orleans" (M.S. thesis, Tulane University School of Social Work, 1947).

CHAPTER VII *Postwar Reforms*

Among the many volumes on Southern history, C. Vann Woodward, *Origins of the New South, 1877–1913* (Baton Rouge: Louisiana State University Press, 1951) was the most helpful as background for this study. See especially Chap. 15 for a fuller discussion of the movements discussed here. The doctoral dissertation (University of North Carolina, 1935) by Lydia Gordon Shivers entitled "The Social Welfare Movement in the South: A Study in Regional Culture and Social Organizations," which included discussion of the influence of religion on Southern welfare movements, was also of interest.

References to the child labor problem include E. J. Murphy, *Problems of the Present South* (New York: Macmillan Co., 1904); A. J. McKelway, "Child Labor in the Southern Cotton Mills," *Annals of the American Academy of Political and Social Science*, XXVI (1906), 256–69; Elizabeth H. Davidson, *Child Labor Legislation in Southern Textile States* (Chapel Hill: University of North Carolina Press, 1939). On industrial social work see Harriet L. Herring, *Welfare Work in Mill Villages* (Chapel Hill: University of North Carolina Press, 1929).

George Washington Cable's address on the lease system before the National Conference of Charities and Corrections in 1883 and "The Freedmen's Case in Equity" appeared in a volume of his work entitled *The Silent South* (New York: Scribner & Co., 1885), followed by *The Negro Question* (New York: Charles Scribner's Sons, 1890). A selection of his writings on civil rights in the South has been issued in a paperback edition under the title *The Negro Question*, ed. Arlin Turner (Doubleday Anchor Books, 1958), and new material from the Cable collection in the Tulane University

Library has been included. For biographical material on Cable see Arlin Turner, *George W. Cable: A Biography* (Durham, N.C.: Duke University Press, 1956). Edmund Wilson in a long review of this biography in the *New Yorker* (November 9, 1957) gives an excellent picture of Cable as a social reformer and an author of note in his period.

Discussions of mental illness among Negroes include William F. Drewry, M.D., "Care and Conditions of the Insane in Virginia," *Proceedings of the National Conference of Charities and Corrections*, 1908, pp. 307–15; Mary O'Malley, M.D., "Psychoses in the Colored Race," *American Journal of Insanity*, LXXI (1914–15), 309–37; E. M. Green, M.D., "Psychoses among Negroes: A Comparative Study," *Journal of Nervous and Mental Diseases*, XLI, No. 11, pp. 697–708.

Useful information on private charities is available in many sources, including *Social Work Yearbook, 1929* (New York: Russell Sage Foundation, 1929); Robert H. Bremner, *From the Depths* (New York: New York University Press, 1956); Frank Watson Dekker, *The Charity Organization Movement in the United States* (New York: Macmillan Co., 1911). Several masters' theses at the Tulane University School of Social Work furnished information about some private agencies in Southern cities: Stella Weber, "A History of Certain Private Charitable Donations in New Orleans" (1935); Anna Berenson, "A Study of the Jewish Children's Home" (1933); Irma M. Isaacson, "A History of Jewish Philanthropy in New Orleans" (1937); Eunice V. Baine, "The History of the Family Service Agency, Memphis, Tennessee" (1942); Minnie Elliott Leeman, "The History of the Family Service Bureau of Houston, Texas, 1904–1943" (1946).

As for the settlement movement in the South the following references are useful: Milton D. Speizman, "The Movement of the Settlement House Idea into the South," *Southwestern Social Science Quarterly*, December, 1963, pp. 257–307; Katharine Hardesty, "Eleanor McMain: Trail Blazer of Southern Social Work" (M.S. thesis, Tulane University School of Social Work, 1936); Bradley Buell, "Eleanor McMain, One of the Pioneers," *Survey Graphic*, January, 1931, pp. 374–77.

CHAPTER VIII *The Social Welfare Conference*

For an account of the origin and development of the National Conference of Charities and Corrections, see Frank J. Bruno, *Trends in Social Work, as Reflected in the Proceedings of the National Conference of Social Work, 1874–1946* (New York: Columbia University Press, 1948). A review of the *Proceedings* themselves is helpful, especially for the years 1878, 1888, 1894, and 1914. Alice R. Hamilton, "The History of the Department of Public Welfare of Georgia, 1919–1937" (M.S. thesis, Tulane University School of Social Work, 1939) also furnishes material on the 1903 Atlanta meeting, as does the journal *Charities*.

The published proceedings of the Southern Sociological Congress constitute the main source of reference for the content of the meetings. All the volumes were edited by James E. McCulloch, who served as secretary of the congress. The titles are *The Call of the New South* (1912), *The South Mobilizing for Social Service* (1913), *Battling for Social Betterment* (1914), *The New Chivalry—Health* (1915), *Democracy in Earnest* (1916), and *Distinguished Service—Citizenship* (1917). Due to war conditions, no proceedings of the congress were published in 1918 or 1919.

For further information on the congress, see Charles E.

Chatfield, "The Southern Sociological Congress: Organization for Uplift," *Tennessee Historical Quarterly*, XIX (1960), 329–47, and his "Southern Sociological Congress: Rationale for Uplift," *Tennessee Historical Quarterly*, XX (1961), 51–64.

INDEX